POETRY NOW

WEST MIDLANDS 1996

Edited by Andrew Head

First published in Great Britain in 1996 by
POETRY NOW
1-2 Wainman Road, Woodston,
Peterborough, PE2 7BU

All Rights Reserved

Copyright Contributors 1995

SB ISBN 1 85731 677 0

FOREWORD

Although we are a nation of poetry writers we are accused of not reading poetry and not buying poetry books: after many years of listening to the incessant gripes of poetry publishers, I can only assume that the books they publish, in general, are books that most people do not want to read.

Poetry should not be obscure, introverted, and as cryptic as a crossword puzzle: it is the poet's duty to reach out and embrace the world.

The world owes the poet nothing and we should not be expected to dig and delve into a rambling discourse searching for some inner meaning.

The reason we write poetry (and almost all of us do) is because we want to communicate: an ideal; an idea; or a specific feeling. Poetry is as essential in communication, as a letter; a radio; a telephone, and the main criteria for selecting the poems in this anthology is very simple: they communicate.

Faced with hundreds of poems and a limited amount of space, the task of choosing the final poems was difficult and as editor one tries to be as detached as possible (quite often editors can become a barrier in the writer-reader exchange) acting as go between, making the connection, not censoring because of personal taste.

In this anthology over two hundred and twenty poems are presented to the reader for their enjoyment.

The poetry is written on all levels; the simple and the complex both having their own appeal.

The success of this collection, and all previous *Poetry Now* anthologies, relies on the fact that there are as many individual readers as there are writers, and in the diversity of styles and forms there really is something to please, excite, and hopefully, inspire everyone who reads the book.

CONTENTS

Untitled	John Chambers	1
Down To The Sea	Norman Cook	1
27 Degrees Sagittarius	Stephen Owen	2
Second World War	Emma Reed	2
City Status	James Kenny	3
Good Friday 1995	Rosamy Murphy	4
Apron Strings	Paul Howard	5
Love At First Sight	M Gouldstone	6
God's Country -		
The Black Country	Alan Dawes	6
Harry	Paul Bowler	7
A Journey Through		
The French Countryside	Ann G Wallace	8
Aldridge In The Fifties	Maurice Birch	9
Time	Peter Chaney	10
The Time Is Now	Karen Asplin	10
D-Day Remembered	Edward Parker	11
Dog At Large	Howard Cooke	12
The Struggle	G A Chapman	13
Shakespeare And Bacon	Snappa	14
Burdened	Shilpe Khanom	15
Thor's Cave I	Chris Thomas	16
A Child's Dream	Gillian Fullbrook	16
Maybe Tomorrow . . .	Nuzhat Asghar	17
The Colosseum, Rome	Brian Harris	18
Cherished Words	Margaret Betts	18
NSRI Ward 23 5/95	Michael Hall	19
Why	Katherine Herbert	20
Trip To London	Marie Barker	20
Night's Defenders	Matthew Hyde	21
My Sister's Birthday	Joan Vincent	22
Poetic Licence	Yvonne Moisey	23
My Grandad	Dorothy Affleck	24
Hatred	Luke Fullbrook	25
Ode To A Country		
Childhood	Beatrice Thorley	26
Unspoilt Scene	Wayne Fisher	26

On Close Inspection	Joan Marlow	28
Perfectly Stained	Elizabeth Watkin	28
My Old Valentine	Dorothy Bassett	29
Cruising	Mary Bonell	30
Phone Call	Michael Cooke	30
A Horrible Day	Linda Taylor	31
Stones	Margaret Cecil Starling	32
Words	June Doolan	33
Dream Lady	Martin Ball	34
A Noisy Hall	Angela Hinde	35
Autonomous Man	Martin Rose	35
Untitled	A Coates	36
The Senses	Peta C C Vale	37
Our Derelict Heritage	Kathleen Bradley	38
Woof-Woof-Woof	Valerie Darby	38
Age	P M Chambers	39
Not So Simple	Vera Lloyd	40
Progress	Anne Livingstone	40
Chinks Of Light . . .	Jean Dooley	41
My Final Words	Louise Sandland	42
The Discreet Affair	Enfys Winter	43
Second Hand Rose	Janet Hancox	44
Two Hearts	Semba Jallow-Rutherford	45
The Ending	Nigath Bi	46
Untitled	A Felgate	46
The Killing Field	Roger Barratt	47
Mother	Bernard Ison	47
White Cider	Richard Parkes	48
Confusion	C A Assam	48
Grow Me Strawberries	Joy Edmunds	49
Orphaned	Nadine Handy	50
21 - Full Circle	Dorothy Ripley	50
The Legacy	Harry Smith	51
Untitled	Florence Carvell	52
A Not So Happy Ending	Yvonne Harrison	52
An Awakening Flower	A Scott	53
Come Outside	Margaret Ensor	54
Extra Curriculum Activity	Josephine Burnett	54

Rain Is Free	Jack Snape	55
Spare Our Children	Stephen McGowan	56
The Stuff That Dreams Are Made Of	Angela Green	57
Untitled	Damian Carter	58
Day's End	F G Sutton	58
Sunny Hollow Lagoon	Peter James O'Rourke	59
Untitled	D McDonald	60
Anniversary	Charles Todd	60
Broken Memories	Bea Evans	61
The Sea	Edna Hunt	62
My Love	Amy Willetts	62
Which	K M Hewitt	63
Time	Patricia Jamieson	64
The Firebird	Debra Davis	64
Happy's Reflection	M Brassington	65
My Daddy	A Fullbrook	65
A Child Alone	Josephine Banks	66
My Benji	May Ward	66
Son	Carol Davies	67
Scorn Me Not	Norman Hancock	68
To My Fellow Dreamers	Fiona Tuckwell	68
Patience	Marie P Holbeche	69
My Immortal Being	Tracey Wiggins	70
Mother	Jan Eyton	70
Untitled	D Stych	71
Seasons	D Fellows	72
Beliefs	A L Price	72
Who Cares?	S A Clay	73
Elephants	Ray Hutchins	74
You Are Mine	Leoni Williams	76
What Is It For?	Philip Carter	76
Cotswold Interlude	Winifred Mustoe	77
Chris And John's Honey	Jean Skitrall	78
If I Should Die	P C Walker	78
Culture In The Sky	Barbara Ann Betts	79
Untitled	D Beecroft	80
Into Stardom	Alyson Faye	80

Title	Author	Page
Seeing	Sandra Holden	81
Superstarmum	P Summerscales	82
Bedd Taliesin - Summer 1995	Susan M Bullock	83
Winter	Adam Henderson	84
March Wind And Summer Sun	William Littleford	85
Pandora Driving	Jane Moreton	86
The Working Man	Tom Grocott	86
Differences	J Watson	87
Life's Like A Thin Golden Thread	Susan Rimmer	88
Knowhere	Shane Glasby	88
Empty Home	Judith Brimble	89
Creation By The Creator	E Wentworth	90
The Stray	Sandra Kozian	90
The Wind	Margaret Westwell	91
I'm Next Door	Laura McNeeney	92
Dilation	Nick Staines	93
Crack	Kenneth Till	94
Lichfield	Jane Redman	94
In Our House	The Fossil	95
What A Mess	Jacqueline Claire Davies	96
The Great Divide	Raymond Baggaley	97
Peer Group Parade	Jill Ison	98
My Dad	Laura Smith	98
Drifting	David Edwards	99
More Than Skin Deep	Daniel Parton	100
Children	Edna Perry	100
My Dear Friend	Jean Beardshore	101
Loneliness	N Gosling	102
Shells On The Hills	Eira Williams	102
Thoughts At Christmas	Gary Westwood	103
When One Becomes Two	C E Hooper	104
The Seagull	Della Roberts	105
Destruction	M A Butcher	106
Christmas Night	Rose Horleston	106
The Lecture	Simon Pennicott	107

Title	Author	Page
Unique	Louise Spears	108
Shaun	K Biggs	108
Stillness	G Thomas	109
A Mother's Love	Susan Hunter	110
My Island	Mary C Soden	111
Mom - Dad	N G Shaw	112
The Visit	Marie Cope	112
Robert	Suzanne Hoare	113
To Joyce	Stephen Poller	114
On The Sleeping Children In Lichfield Cathedral	Jean Quance	114
Plates	Margaret A Stonier	115
Prosthetics	David Ellerton (Deceased)	116
The Book	Mark Hipwell	117
Reality And Sympathy	Julian Devereux	118
Urban Fox	Amelia Canning	118
Hiroshima	Kate Herd	119
November Incident	J Curlett	120
The Agonies Of Deception	Chris Davies	120
A Short Extract Of Life	Kulbir Sharni	121
Snooty Swans	Joan Ierston	122
Linen	Paul Coles	122
Small Wonder	Elizabeth E Smullen	123
Twilight	Tony Smith	124
The World As One	Dave 'Snapper' Snape	125
Certified Insane	Rita Pal	126
Death Of A Family Dog	M C Eggleton	127
An Album For Christmas	Mary Hyland	128
Door To Door Salesmen	E Taylor	129
Sexth Column	Alan N Marshall	129
My Best Friend	Ann Marie Hinds	130
Maternal Gratitude	Steven McLuckie	130
Writer's Block	Alison Walters	131
Grains	Dennis Marshall	132
Rediscovering Lollipop Sticks	Emma Purshouse	133
The Smile	L S King	134
The Changing Seasons	Jackie Thornton	135

Perfunctory Factories Mechanical Men	David Vanter	136
Lament Of The Universe	Dorothy Bell-Hall	136
The Word	Paul Williams	137
Deafness	Sandra Bache	138
Roll . . . Up . . . The . . . Flag	Dennis Parkes Rowley Regis	138
My Garden Of Friendship	Mary Amelia Payne	139
The Five Senses	Theo James	140
My City	Joan McAvoy	141
A Wartime Christmas	John Hoose	142
Church Rally	Cecilia Simpson	143
A Love That's Not Returned	Richard Ball	143
The Government	Rachel Freestone	144
War	C D Wells	145
The Waiting Room	D Tinson	145
Dreaming In A Dream	Abdul Rob	146
My Dream Cottage	Cynthia Shum	147
Ironed Out	Keith Melbourne	148
The Oak Tree	I Griffiths	148
Home To Me	Mary Morrison	149
No Greater Gift	Ken Clifford	150
Anniversary	Evelyn M Harding	150
To A Hippopotamus At Mzima	Lena Brewe	151
Brain Juice Flan	Mark Underwood	152
Unfortunate	Y Malone	152
My Ruling Passion	Rachel Cefai	153
Parties!	Geraldine Squires	154
Second-Hand Rose	Lee Chidlow	154
In Autumn Winds	Graham Roberts	155
Afterwards	Kerri Goodhead	156
Old And Decrepit	Jane Holmes	157
The Twentieth Century	K W Benoy	158
The Time Of My Life	L B Lingard	159
Irresponsible Sea	Eleanor Clifford	160
A Lighthouse Shines?	Steve B	160
A New Way	Frances Greves	161
A Tiger's Tale	S A Ward	162

Adrift	Michael Dowd	162
Enchantment	Clare Hill	163
Untitled	Sibyl Smith	164
Another Time, Another Place	Sheila Corbett	165

UNTITLED

When I started as a boy
My heart was always full of joy
I worked harder then
Than as a signalman
No chief clerk piling on the work
A cabin of my own to work
Seeing people to business bent
I had safely sent
When on 12 hours, I saw them
Homeward bound was their intent
No Christmas present for me
Looking out of my window to see
Doors are fast, no wheels skidding
Now retired, I'm not kidding.

John Chambers

DOWN TO THE SEA

We went down to the sea,
Sat on the beach for tea.
The tide did flow,
The water aglow,
Reflecting the shining sun,
On its orbital run.

We went home from the sea,
In a car, you and me,
With carbon monoxide to breathe.
On a road could not leave.
So much for the sea.
Now stay home for tea.

Norman Cook

27 DEGREES SAGITTARIUS

Sixteen rockets pointing at the moon
I've found a girl
I can really love.

Sixteen rockets pointing at the moon
I flew above my launchers
years ago.

Sixteen rockets pointing at the moon
my eyes are ultra-violet
my lips infra-red.

Sixteen rockets pointing at the moon
my brain is a transmitting station
broadcasting from the centre of the galaxy
27 degrees Sagittarius.

Stephen Owen

SECOND WORLD WAR

Spring used to be a happy time,
Eucalyptus trees would grow,
Cold it is now,
Old and dull,
Now there is no happiness,
Death is all we see.

War is the cause,
Oh how cruel and dreadful,
Really, really sad,
Lamb used to be for Sunday lunch,
Dried egg is now that special treat.

War isn't right,
After all, we're all human,
Rivalry will only kill this world!

Emma Reed (11)

CITY STATUS

The Yards all have surrendered to breakers,
The roar of rivets no longer survive,
No red dust-covered caulkers or boilermakers
No harmonising Yard hooters at five.

No mass exodus now floods neighbouring streets
To clamber on board waiting buses and trams,
Standing empty in line before filling all seats;
Some meet mums pushing high Silver Cross prams.

Paper, clothing, coalmining, glassmaking,
Shipyards in their entirety, all are now gone.
Staiths from which ships would be loaded, once taking
Coal from twenty five mines - now but one.

'More Coal!' 'More Ships!' was the exhortation,
'Your endeavours will provide Post-War fruits;'
No coalmines, no shipyards, no job expectations,
But betrayal by the men in grey suits.

Three hundred years with a Harbour and Port;
Record shipping produced during two World Wars.
The largest shipbuilding town in the world is now nought
But a city manufacturing Japanese cars.

James Kenny

GOOD FRIDAY 1995

Was the world beautiful as you left the city?
Was there early morning freshness as you trudged up the hill?
Was the grass rainbowed with dewdrops as the cross splintered into your shoulders?
Were the birds chorusing the air with melodies?
Or were the sounds of your creation drowned out with the clanking of chains,
With the measured tread of footsteps and the raucousness of jeers?
Did you notice the morning freshness,
Or did the dust churned up by marching feet pollute the air you breathed?
Did the sun's rays gently warm your skin,
Or did intolerable heat and effort furrow sweat across your brow?

Could you hold the beauty and the sheer pain and distress
In some dancing dynamic,
Interplay of exultation and drowning sorrow,
Or were you, like us, just too overwhelmed to cope?
Out of depth in a sea of anguish?
Unable to do anything but gasp,
Just drag on,
No awareness other than the unbearable intolerableness of it all?

You have been there before us Lord,
Wherever the Calvary road leads us.
You are not a distant God,
But a foot-weary traveller with us.
Hold our hands as we walk this road,
Wipe our brows,
Help us up when we fall,
Not just a shining example to follow,
But an enabling presence,
So we can just keep travelling,
Knowing you will pick us up,
To carry us when we can't cope any longer.

Rosamy Murphy

APRON STRINGS

Threatening, simmering. Boiling, spurting pans.
Spitting frying pans and hissing pressure cookers.
The child wide eyed watches the war zone, fearful
Of the enemies which crouch on the hobs,
Waiting to pounce with their scolding claws
Upon her vulnerable flesh.

But, amongst the steam of the battle
A tall goddess keeps them in control,
Her hands gliding through the steel,
Lifting lids, changing the heat, stirring,
Adding salt; a thousand jobs at once
With the ease of a warm knife through butter;
A hum dancing from her lips born by a smile,
There is nothing she can't handle.

The child runs to her legs, hugs them, afraid,
As the war rages all around her, unrelenting.
Mother's soothing voice accompanied by her fingers,
Stroking comfort into her; calming the fear
Which beats in her innocent heart.
Apron strings reaching out; two cords to hold,
As mother returns to the task in hand.
But with the desire to please mother stronger,
She returns to the sanctuary of the living room,
Where daddy sits, watching the television.

Paul Howard

LOVE AT FIRST SIGHT

That special day I met you
I saw you standing alone,
Before I even knew your name
I called you love.
In my heart I knew.
There could never be another you.
We spent such happy days together
Every moment treasured oh, so few,
The sun always shone with you there
The thought of never seeing you again
Was too hard to bear,
You left this life we had to part
But you will always live in my heart
Please wait for me my special love
Oh dearest friend.

M Gouldstone

GOD'S COUNTRY - THE BLACK COUNTRY

Years ago when life was hard,
When folk wore Sunday best
People shared an enclosed yard,
And the Sabbath was for rest.

Latches, keys and locks were formed,
This still occurs today,
Money scarce, items pawned,
Credit had no say!

Saddles were sewn by tradesmen's hands,
This still goes on today,
Glass was blown by artisans,
Sculptured in a unique way.

Coal was picked, some used a spade,
Does this occur today?
From coalfield tips, bricks were made,
Formed from coloured clay.

God's Country wore the nation's crown,
An industrious shining jewel,
With chain and anchors of renown,
The miners earned England's fuel.

Alan Dawes

HARRY

If you're coming to play can you come alone
Please don't bring Harry, he's best left at home
I've never met no-one like him he's the nastiest of boys.
He pulls your hair and kicks your shins and breaks all your toys
He will shove your head down the pan, then he'll pull the chain
Last week when he borrowed my bike it came back without any trace of paint.
And if we play at marbles he'll push them up my nose
And if I try to run away he stamps upon my toes
Yesterday to top it all he pinched my brand new ball,
He broke my tennis racket and banged my head against the wall.
So you see I've had enough I just can't take no more
I'm battered and bruised and also very sore.
So if you're coming to play today can you come alone
Please don't bring Harry he's best left at home.

Paul Bowler

A JOURNEY THROUGH THE FRENCH COUNTRYSIDE

Nature, your patchwork quilt displayed,
In shades of green,
As fields that stretch for miles,
Play host, to sunflowers bright,
Who bow their heads,
As if in some majestic prayer,
A tractor glides the land it tills,
Infertile as a virgin awaiting conception,

Rape seed lays a carpet gold,
Whilst the crop sprayer, toils relentlessly on,
Dusk falls, pink tinges fill the sky,
Symmetrical patterns etched upon the land,
Rivers green, that mirror the sky,
As they wind through banks of trees,
Swirling bands, of yellow and brown,
Sunflowers, like spinning tops of old,

Trees dot the landscape, in silhouette,
As night time drops her dark, and empty cloak,
Lights appear, scattered across the land,
Cities in the distance, give a twinkling display,
Neon lights beckon from off the motorway,
Enticing the tired, and hungry,
Nature, your world hidden for a while,
Until the light of dawn, once more, her switch,
To throw.

Ann G Wallace

ALDRIDGE IN THE FIFITIES

I remember when we swam
Below the Withy Dam
By an old tin shack
And a chimney stack
In a field of Marjoram.

And within a half a mile
Of the Aldridge brick and tile.
You could feel the draught
From an old mine shaft
If you tarried there a while.

On the road to Walsall Wood
Grew a tree with a sticky bud
Whilst in the middle of a stream
Stood an evergreen
Which thrived in a pool of mud

In the quarry beneath the ridge
To the south side of Aldridge
We would often sit
In an old clay pit
A throw from the Donkey Bridge.

On pit mounds we would play
By a disused railway.
Or like cat and mouse
Round the old pump house
We dallied the time away.

Maurice Birch

TIME

Where are you time, I know you're there,
Relentlessly going your way,
Leading me to the future, where
The past is one second away.

Are you so right, am I so wrong,
That you must keep ahead of me,
Taking me from, where I belong,
To somewhere, I don't want to be.

For you and I both share my fate,
We could both make a lifetime last,
But you could never be that late,
And abandon hope with the past.

In your inexorable pace,
I become defenceless and age,
And move from this positive place,
Towards the uncertain stage.

Time, where are you leading me to,
Will you be resolute, until
The moment comes when I meet you,
On the day that Time will stand still.

Peter Chaney

THE TIME IS NOW

My mommy said it's time for bed
When the little hand is on the seven
But they stay up till it's really dark
And the little hand is on the eleven.

My baby sister sleeps most of the day
And often wakes for a change of nappy
She's too young to know of time
As long as she's fed and cuddled she's happy.

When it's summer why can't it snow?
Why does daddy start work at 7 o'clock?
What's the big thing about time - I don't know
And why when you're late, your wages they'll dock.

Karen Asplin

D-DAY REMEMBERED

Me? I saw your face through fifty years.
I watched those men in reminiscence and fear.
I saw bravery and pain, and bought the stamps
An old boy lost and falling,
As he hit the ground - I thought of you
I never witnessed D-Day, just
A celebration or two, only another history that
I'll probably now know.
But I never lost sight of you.
Ancient sights like Utah, a State
I believe, I feel, that is history
And claimed in eternity.
Though in memories and any emotion say
It feels too long ago.

Edward Parker

DOG AT LARGE

Dear Madam or Sir, have you noticed a change
In your Fido's demeanour of late,
Is it old age, distemper, a touch of the mange
Or not enough food on his plate?
Could it be that he's been disappointed in love,
That his lady-love's got a new beau.
Has some mongrel discovered his bone treasure trove
And scavenged the lot, at one go?
Unwisely, perhaps, you have caused the upset
By neglecting to make any fuss
And bestowing your love on another new pet,
A sly, slinky, saturnine puss.
Or maybe a budgie, a slick, talking bird
To which you continually chat,
So that faithful old Fido gets hardly a word;
No welcome for him on the mat.
Whatever the reason, there isn't a doubt
He has lost quite a lot of his charm,
His department is that of a poor down-and-out,
His attitude spreads some alarm
To postmen who thought of your dog as a friend,
That his bark wasn't prelude to bite,
But now a chance meeting is likely to end
With man in undignified flight.
Your postman advises, Dear Madam or Sir,
That letters will not now appear,
More bites from your now unpredictable cur
Could possibly blight his career!

Howard Cooke

THE STRUGGLE

The gossamer thread of the spider web stretched out like a pattern in lace
Hovering like a wheel of glass, suspended in outer space.
Patiently and motionless its architect lay in wait.
For all the insects of winged flight to land on its dinner plate
As the sun dropped beneath the horizon, night creatures began to stir.
Moving in trepidation, aware of the need for care.
Attracted by a glowing light a cranefly succumbs automatic.
Dancing like a drunken man so wild and erratic.
Closer and closer the cranefly flew towards its date with fate.
Blind to the lurking danger as it searched for a receptive mate.
Attracted by a nearby light as dusk spread its deepening gloom.
Its gossamer wings touched the gossamer web announcing the cranefly's
                                                                                                             doom.
Signals from the cranefly's struggle alerted the spider to its plight.
Creating a life - death drama to be enacted through the night
Like an athlete bursting from the blocks the spider moved at pace.
To cross its web and seize its prey in a deadly powerful embrace.
In its realisation its life end was near the cranefly attempted escape.
Its chances slim its future grim as its final moments took shape.
The spiders bite into the body of the cranefly signalled the end.
Unable to fight its enemy unable to defend.
Anaesthetised the cranefly ceased its struggle to survive.
Cocooned in silk for a later date, mummified, still alive.
Placed in the spiders larder the encounter finally through.
It left just one more thing that night the spider had got to do.
Repair its web before the dawn and secrete itself from sight.
To hide away throughout the day prepare once more for the night.

G A Chapman

SHAKESPEARE AND BACON

Shakespeare was Dyslexic.
I'll think you'll find it's true.
He was brilliant at poetry,
But at spelling he hadn't a clue.

But this did not dishearten him,
He still wrote his books and plays,
Though a lot of people laughed at him,
In those pre-Shakespearian days.

Till a man called Francis Bacon,
Said to Shakespeare, 'I say will,
How come your spelling is so bad,
When your content is so brill?'

Shakespeare shrugged his shoulders,
And said, 'Maybe it's just I'm thick',
(For in those days no-one had heard
Of being Dyslexic).

So bacon helped old shaky,
To revamp all his text,
First correcting spelling mistakes,
Then punctuation next.

Now Shakespeare is respected,
His books and plays still sell,
And no-one really knows or cares,
That the man could never spell.

So if you are Dyslexic,
Don't let them laugh at you,
For with a little help,
You could become a Shakespeare too.

Snappa

BURDENED

Today I saw him again,
such swiftness and elegance,
graced his walk.
But cautious he was of me,
when he saw, and I wanted to talk.

He must have by now, sensed that I have feelings
for him,
though my parents may call it thoughts of blatant sin.
Sadly he may have reason to believe that
my feelings are based on a mere crush,
but every time I see him I get a sensational rush.

Having him in my thoughts is becoming unbearable for me,
I've got to let him know, to see if it's meant to be.

I cannot help wandering if my feelings are an impossible dream,
Which will fall at all aspects,
and tear at the seams,
or could my dream become reality?
Blatant impossibility turning to the only way.
I know the odds are against me, so all I can do is pray.

After I tell him about how I feel,
he'll probably stay away,
thinking I'm not for real,
thinking I'm too young,
not being able to experience love.
Why doesn't God help me, in his throne up above.
I wish that my mind wasn't burdened,
with these emotions I feel.
When will my heart and mind be free,
when will the wounds heal.

Shilpe Khanom (16)

THOR'S CAVE I

This skylined limestone, barely grey. Rock
Ribcage strains, breathtaking. A neck-stretch
Incline, climbs beyond on leaf-fleshed scaffold.

Regarding land and sky, skeleton's
Apotheosis, fossil framed with
Weathered face, always asking mouth and maw.

Bleaching bones laid bare by blood-eagle
Erosion. Lime lightens, calcium
Carbonate hard. Sea body, stiff with time.

Crag's clouded thought rumours cumulus.
Thor's Cave echoes earth and air unheard.
Water coursed and cut this mouth; washed out, crammed

With landscape's memories. Stone stories
In strata. Morphology described
By discourse, mapped by land-locked metaphor.

Object that experience owns. Not
Self possessed by name. Charted nature
Tamed by tongue, claims contracting space to place.

Across imagined contours, map's signs
Make sense. Like the back of my hand
Land lays, corporeal cartography.

Chris Thomas

A CHILD'S DREAM

To every child there comes a need
To have a world of make-believe
Where toffee apples grow on trees
And the moon is really made of cheese
Where witches stir their evil brew
But a good fairy will rescue you.

When snuggly in their beds they lie
They dream of monsters in the sky
Where little elves and gnomes come round
When the air around is filled with
Sweet melodic sound.

After night, another day when once
Again the child will play
At pirates who will sail the seas
Of highway men and robberies
Where he will always come off best
'Tis a pity this dream cannot be kept.

Gillian Fullbrook

MAYBE TOMORROW ...

You say you love me,
You say you really do,
You say you're mine forever,
but is that true?
How do I know
what kind of person you are
You seemed all right at first,
but that was from far.
Maybe tomorrow,
Your feelings will change,
Maybe tomorrow,
You'll see me as strange,
Maybe tomorrow,
Your love will end,
Maybe tomorrow,
You won't even see me as a friend.

Nuzhat Asghar

THE COLOSSEUM, ROME

Ten million stones recall
Ten thousand souls whose anguished cries
Of Victory, arose from this arena.

For such contempt that man had shown
He trod the path of pain.
Surmounting human weakness yet again.

He led the way through just such vales
And with two thousand years now gone
We dwell upon such Grace.

Oh, silent ruin! Recall in man
The challenge that faced Him.
Tear-out the libertine within, renew this Temple's face.

Let us turn once more to Him,
Not for pleasure, nor for gain,
But for Grace, that we may clearly see our destiny.

Let us tread the path of pain with charity.
A stone now turned
For Calvary.

Brian Harris

CHERISHED WORDS

An old letter to treasure
Silent thoughts which give much pleasure
Inspiring words to cherish with care
Thoughtfulness that was always there
From a loved one to another
An old letter from mother.

Margaret Betts

NSRI WARD 23 5/95
(ANTHENA AND THE CENTAUR)

He thought it was a wet November in Wales
And when the time that heals dimmed the light,
He politely asked what time the show started.
Keith looked blank, no-one had told him anything.

For Andrew I had come in a plane, with his wife.
Too late for the bar, half way into Keith's story.
Jet lagged I lay and listened, simply knowing that
I could pick up Keith's threads next time around.

I could see, window ledged, a school posed photo
Of two children, snap. Eyes dormant to the lens
As though all this was preordained at the click.
Keith was told not to love his baby, it died at six months.

We were all running in an hourglass of confusion.
I felt like an interloper, not worthy of cries or help.
Treading around the edges of this cathedral conspiracy,
Helping to dust Keith down along with everyone else.

Did I really want to play in their shadowy dreams?
Dancing to Bon Jovi in some Iberian bodega or
Huddled two as one, warm arms under cold sheets.
The Centaur stamped a dust and turned, leaving

Andrew to gather and kindle his family of memories,
Keith to re-string the tightrope, this time over the fence.
And Odysseus-like I fled laughing with my wife
Whilst David came in on a breeze to fight for his life.

Michael Hall

WHY

She walks down the street,
Hair laden with flowers,
Face overflowing with beauty,
Suddenly, it changes,
They grab at her,
They throw the flowers from her hair,
And replace them with mud,
Her face,
Once warm and glowing,
Now tear stained and dirty,
Her clothes ripped to shreds,
She stands there sobbing,
Passers by, pass by,
Ignoring her discomfort,
Little children stare in amazement,
Or shout to their mothers,
'Look at her mum!'
They shout,
Look at her over there,
Do the people stop to ask if she wants help?
No,
And all because she is *black*.

Katherine Herbert (13)

TRIP TO LONDON

There's a light at the end of the tunnel
As we travel to old London town
We are on a train with a large funnel
and steam and smoke are going up and down.

The white of the steam and grey of smoke
Covers all the front of the train
It covers all the window popping folk
Not to mention the wheels and panes.

As we pull into the station
We hear the sound of the horn
It sounds as though all creation
is born on this good morn!

Marie Barker

NIGHT'S DEFENDERS

Not everything that comes out at night is evil.
Take the stars, and the moonlight,
And the guardian angels,
Who watch over children while they sleep.
Even in a world of shadows,
The light still shines through the darkness,
And the birds still sing and the children still play,
And the shadows can never engulf the light,
Not while one good thought exists,
Either in the conscience of humanity
Or in the realms of fantasy.
So, while evil tries to rule the night,
The stars, and the moonlight, and the angels remain,
The Guardians of Twilight.
Because not everything that comes out at night is evil.

Matthew Hyde

MY SISTER'S BIRTHDAY

A happy birthday sister dear
Your one a year day's come
Make the most of every hour
You have much more than some.

I hope it's a bright and sunny day
And it makes you feel alive
Tucked up in your little bungalow
You'll want to have a jive.

I hope the old weather cock is facing your way
And he wants to have a natter
And when your phone rings on the day
It's your sister wants to chatter.

I hope you'll have a lot of cards
All wishing you greetings sincere
Happy birthday sister Pat
Another birthday is here.

And when at the very end of the day
And you're tucked up in your bed
You'll feel so quietly happy
Congrats ringing in your head.

However quietly you celebrate
It's still your one day dear
So happy birthday sister Pat
These wishes are sincere.

Joan Vincent

POETIC LICENCE

Stop Larkin' about with words!
Like a Mole, discard the waste
as you burrow to the roots of thought.

You Auden't to be a big Spender
of language; that could Causley
-gitimate complaint that your skill's
on the Wain. You might go Amis,
or Abse-nt from poetic circles
for good. Get some Beer inside you
(or perhaps a Porter would carry you
out of the mire?) Enright
with thrifty care.

    Follow
a Patten of perfection and weave
the Silkin strands of experience
into a banner of truth
as bright as Joseph's coat
of many colours.

    Fly
the pennant high; prepare
your tight craft to the last
nail and let the Smith
hammer the point home.
Site a Gunn for defence
from the Hughes and cries of a mind
storm-tossed. Take the Tiller,
steer by the Logue-star
and Sail to the heart of your meaning.

Yvonne Moisey

MY GRANDAD

My grandad's horse was big and black
His nostrils flared, his eyes rolled back.
He stamped his hooves in such a way,
Never could he be child's play.

My grandad's goose was large and white
Protected his house with an almighty bite
He hissed and spat at all he saw,
And chased intruders from the door.

My grandad's pigs were fat and pink
Their house was dark and such a stink
They honked and screamed no means like ladies
But how sweet their little babies.

My grandad's goat was as tall as me
Kind and gentle he was not meant to be
He ate the washing from the line
And everything he knew was mine.

My grandad was short and stout
And at his animals would never shout
He wore an old jacket and flat cap
Every afternoon he took a nap.

He taught me much about old ways
And never quoted good old days
He lived till he was eighty five
But oh! How I wish he were still alive.

Dorothy Affleck

HATRED

I felt the thunderstorm brewing
in my head
This other Eden was just a useless lie
I need help, I feel confused.
The pain my heart felt was for you

You stretch me out so you can put
me down
You dry me out so you can force me
to drown
You knock me down when I'm back on
my feet.

Truth lies in trails of guilt
Tweak me clean, left in agony
She really loves to break me in two
This parasite will not follow you.

You stretch me out so you can
pin me down
You starve me so you can force me
to eat
Hatred is all that keeps me alive
You cover my mouth when I try
to scream

I will survive, you will not
suffocate me.

Luke Fullbrook (17)

ODE TO A COUNTRY CHILDHOOD

Happy was I as a country child;
Free as a bird in the woodlands wild.
My garden - the meadow ablaze with bright flowers,
And a sparkling stream where I whiled away hours.

My music - the songbirds, the drone of the bees,
The patter of raindrops, the sigh on the breeze.
My perfume - may blossom and the fresh smell of pine,
Wild honeysuckle and sweet eglantine.

My playmates - the children from the valley nearby.
Our pastimes gave pleasure no money could buy.
We paddled in streamlets and romped in the hay,
And revelled in snowdrifts on a bright winter's day.

The wonder of nature held us in its thrall:
We considered the ants, so wise yet so small;
And the tiniest seeds which, with soil, sun and showers,
Like magic burst forth into green leaves and flowers.

Then when day turned to darkness with awe we would scan
The vast Universe, beyond reach of man -
Overwhelming, mysterious, all part of one plan.

Beatrice Thorley

UNSPOILT SCENE

As I stroll in the shade
  Of the towering oak trees,
The mighty twisted branches
  And the emerald sky of leaves.
Branches entwine, kissed heavily with deep green leaf
  So that through them no ray of sun shall ever peep.

The ground upon which I tread
    So dense and so thick,
An entangled mass of ferns and bushes,
    Wild grass and stick.
Silence prevails
    Then the snap of a twig
A squirrel busily searches for food that once he has hid.

I follow a track that has been worn well with time
    A light breeze whispers, carrying the fresh scent of pine
Through the trees I see glimmers of light
    Then piercing through the branches
Attacking the shade,
    Are rays of light like long golden blades.

Then out of the darkness and into the light,
    Into the lush green meadow
Where the sun burns bright.
    The birds are singing
The mood is uplifting,
    Butterflies dance with the wild flowers

Here I stand
    Enchanted by nature's wondrous powers.
Here I rest
    For hours and hours
Forgetting the city
    Forgetting the smoke
And the war torn nations that have no hope.

These must be the scenes that God had planned
    Before he put man upon this land.

Wayne Fisher

ON CLOSE INSPECTION

I teach you the secrets:
Long division, grammar,
Of people long ago,
Rivers, mountains, snow.
And in return you give
The view of a daisy head
The wonder of a soap bubble
The certain knowledge you tell
That tomorrow, all will be well.

My gift to you seems mean,
Your gift to me is rich.
But the world values much more
The raw examination score.

Yet architect ant in his elaborate hill
Never had to swallow the assessment pill.
And children from your ant perspective
You have true knowledge, not reflective.
So why do I cloud your clear view
With uneasy facts piled onto you?

Still fix your clear and youthful eye
On the bright daisies and the starry sky.
Perfect vision is your temporary view,
Don't let me take it too soon from you.

Joan Marlow

PERFECTLY STAINED

Short is the night, long is the day,
I remember asking if you were going my way.
I was blue, same as you,
Always wondering what you were going to say.

White is your skin, dark are your veins,
I remember clutching, as it started to rain.
Holding my throat, I grab your coat,
Short is my life and I'm still perfectly stained.

Elizabeth Watkin

MY OLD VALENTINE

Tired after work.
Relaxing in your chair.
I realise how much you mean to me
As I watch you sleeping there.

Our first flush of youth is over.
The years have come and gone,
But still you are as dear to me
As the day God made us one.

Glasses slipping off your nose.
Your hair is thinning now.
Laughter lines around your eyes,
And furrows on your brow.

But as I sit and gaze at you
And look back down the years.
I think of all the things we've shared.
Our joys, our hopes and fears.

I do not need cards and things,
Or to even wine and dine.
For I will always love you.
My dear old Valentine.

Dorothy Bassett

CRUISING

Many folk say that nothing is finer,
Than a voyage aboard an ocean liner.
Ladies wear jewels, evening dress.
Decor, drinks, dining, certainly impress.

Others prefer a yacht with sails,
The excitement, the glamour, never fails.
Sunbathing on deck, or if it should rain,
Some music or puzzles to test the brain.

There's so much to do when you're afloat,
So many enjoyments, whatever the boat.
It is so convenient, no daily packing,
Everything available, nothing lacking.

But best of all, taken by and large,
Is the lazy journey by canal barge.
Animals, birds, pass by in flocks,
It's even fun to assist at locks.

Energetic folk on the towpath may walk,
While others just sit, enjoying a talk.
When you're feeling low, at the end of your tether,
It's great on a barge, whatever the weather.

Mary Bonell

PHONE CALL

When old friends die not yet three score and ten
It gets you round to thinking you could be joining them,
Plucked before your time; a grandpa not to be
Thought about it yesterday when you spoke to me.

Then I thought of something else that took away all fear
What we have will live forever, distance brings us near;
Friends . . . Always, never any more
Guess I will wait at the golden gate to even up the score.

Till then kindred spirits, occasional conversations with no time,
To wonder why we never did at your place or at mine.
A lost friend, a phone call, triggered off my thought;
Perhaps we should not dial again? Unless you think we ought.

Michael Cooke

A HORRIBLE DAY

The day I laid my friend to rest.
Brought great pain to my chest,.
To hold her to my heart, to say goodbye.
Watch those beautiful eyes fade and die.
My heart it heaved, my lips prayed.
I prayed to the Lord, don't take her away.
With eyes filled with tears and a rock in my throat
My head felt as though it wanted to float.
The best little Pal, that I ever knew.
Opened her wings once more, and to heaven she flew.

My little pal was a bird called Billy.
She was like a child although it sounds silly.
We laughed and talked and sang together.
She would make me happy, no matter what weather
But to put her in my hat that day!
Her resting place a hole of clay.
Oh yes! What a horrible day.

Linda Taylor

STONES

From Scotland's highest mountain
Down to England's southern shore
You will find lots of stones.
You'll find them by the score.

Moorland towns of ancient stone,
Smooth pavements in the street,
Cobbles in the Market Square
Where the people meet.

Pillars tall and tracery fine
Of Cathedrals and Churches.
Fine statues in the parks
Flanked by flowers and birches.

Cairns in remote places.
Elgin statues of marble.
Monoliths at Stonehenge
At which people marvel.

Pebbles on the Chesil Beach
Large down to small shingle.
Groynes reaching out to sea
Where surf and sea-weed mingle.

Millstone grit of the Pennine ridge,
Semi-precious gems and workmen's homes,
Pebbles in the babbling brooks.
They are stones, just stones!

Margaret Cecil Starling

WORDS

I met a man on a country road, his hair was long, his clothes
were old!
His skin was brown, with a weathered look, but his smile was warm,
So a chance I took to speak to him!
He did not ask for much in life, just a kindly word, but no advice.
'I enjoy my life, it is so free, it's the life I chose, and is good to me.
I've got no wealth, and possess no home, through this beautiful
land, I love to roam! People I meet are very kind!'
These are the words he left behind.

I met a youth! In a busy town, his skin was pale, and he wore
a frown!
His dress was smart, his stance was straight
So a chance I took to speak to him!
'He told me he had travelled far, to visit many foreign lands
Never had to take a job! To spoil his un-worked precious hands!'
But he wore no smile, he knew no love, no beauty did he see.
He was the only one in mind
Those are the words he left behind.

I met a child! By an old Church gate, with curly hair and a
dirty face.
Where the tears had run, they had left their mark.
So a chance I took to speak to him.
With a little sob, and a gasp for breath, he gently spoke of
his mother's death.
'I come to visit every day, and tell her of my love,
She isn't very far away, she lives with God in the heavens above.
But one day we shall meet again, how lovely that will be!
And now some flowers I must find!'
These are the words he left behind.

June Doolan

DREAM LADY

The rain fell over me.
Shattering my sanity.
I was lonely, cordoned off.
From the world and its vanity.

I saw my girl one day,
Suspended amongst the cloud.
Down you came, entering my life,
Dressed angelically in a pure white shroud.

I can't describe the feeling you gave me,
Hovering gently over the grass towards -
A man who felt suspended in a dream,
But all too happy to look forwards.

Take my hand and walk the corridors of life
Together, or trap yourself behind the bars of time.
It's your choice, my beauty, my love,
My darling cherry. Please be mine.

Your hair scatters in the wind,
Like grassy crops in a healthy, green field,
Your blue eyes mesmerise my soul,
It spirals upward, and lands healed.

Please say yes and make me happy.
Happy like the birth of a baby.
Smiling like a clown who really means it,
Like a man, grabbed and controlled, may be -
By love for my dream lady.

Martin Ball

A NOISY HALL

A teacher in The Hall
Shouts at us all,
Sit down, shut up and get on with your work.

In that school there is that hall
Still the noisiest of all.

The class room next door
is the quietest of all,
No shouting, no screaming,
No knock at the door,
No squeaking of chairs,
No teachers talking.
I wish I was in that class,
but will it last?

Angela Hinde (12)

AUTONOMOUS MAN

The sun's dusty rays
filter through the blackened sky lights
piercing the industrial haze.
Here, works autonomous man
Blank mechanical gaze.

Blindly working in line
not caring
each movement a study in time
hopelessly dreaming his tomorrows
and never able to climb
from a reality that fetters his mind.

Martin Rose

UNTITLED

Another pensive, cynical prose begins
To the reader, it may enhance futile dreams
As the writer, it is my pen, my version. . .
It is dawn, the light of life, warmth envelops the soul
Shady characters go about their business
The beaches begin to fill
The priest kneels and prays, carefully, precisely
Commuters take their desks, clock in
The morning is warm, the flowers enjoy
Mother nature tends to her kingdom, she knows
The breeze is faint, almost extinct
The musician in the subway strums away, again
Two men chatter away on the network
Nobody notices the sky, too busy, don't care.
It doesn't concern me, it is destiny
The mother collects her child from school
In the country lane, the cows wait for milking
The traffic builds on the roads
Nobody hears the men finish on the network
They are silent, still, exhausted
Life one moment, then nothing
The decision was made, the buttons pushed
Only God is busy now, counting the souls,
And yet, the Devil is ecstatic
He waited a long time for man's destruction.

A Coates

THE SENSES

Such beauty is visible to the naked eye,
The greenness of grass, so many blues in the sky,
The spots on a ladybird, the stripes on a bee,
The shape of leaves differ on every tree,
The colours of the spectrum, each and every shade,
Without sight to a lifeless grey would fade.

A loving word whispered in our ear
A tuneful melody we would not hear.
The whirl and swirl from the washing machine.
The hiss of an iron angrily letting off steam.
The tick-tock of the clock, the chirp of a bird,
All these everyday sounds would pass unheard.

The loving touch, the gentle caress,
The contours of the face would be meaningless
Without the sense of touch. The prick of a thorn;
The soft, coldness of snow; a flame that is warm;
A rough skinned peach; a nectarine's smooth peel,
Without touch these textures we just could not feel.

Wherever we go, each day we are faced
With numerous foods to try and to taste.
Freshly smoked salmon; the richness of goose;
The sharpness of olives; peaches oozing with juice;
A lemon so sharp; a strawberry so sweet,
It's the taste that makes food so pleasurable to eat.

Oh, to smell the meadow on a fine summer's day;
Or newly mown grass and bales of cut hay;
Freshly ground coffee; or newly baked bread;
Sensuous perfumes; or flowers in a bed.
A joint being roasted and bacon being fried.
All these simple pleasures our senses provide.

Peta C C Vale

OUR DERELICT HERITAGE

The sad face of it
looks out dismally over
the murky canal. For miles
there are decaying pottery-
factories - the few remaining
bottle kilns stand. . . forgotten.
An era snuffed out; erased,
removed, eradicated,
Suppressed into the bottom
of progress's shoe.
'My grandad used to work there,
as a 'Saggamakers bottom knocker'.
It was a hard job, but
at least he had one.'
The sad, sad face of it;
windowless, soul-less factories
line the khaki coloured waters
that people now sit
and fish out of or walk
their doggies along:
pleasant enough: except
for the barren pottery factories
sadly watching as you go by.

Kathleen Bradley

WOOF-WOOF-WOOF

I am a border collie
My coat is black and white
If you think you have heard me
You would probably be right.

Woof woof woof! Is all I can say
To make myself understood.
You know I would ask for a biscuit or bone
And I'd say please if I could.

It's very frustrating for a dog you know
Not to be able to speak
I have to make a lot of noise
When your attention I seek.

So next time you hear your dog bark
Think about what I have said
It's only trying to talk to you
It probably needs to be fed.

Valerie Darby

AGE

It's a frightening thing this growing old
You must be forward and bold
Remember all the good things both done and said
Look with confidence to the road ahead
God willing we will all get there
That's the time to sit and stare.

Stare at the beauty of all things around
Things that cannot be valued by the pound
Remembering family and friends so dear
The one's that always bought a cup of cheer

And as I come to the end of life's road
It will be time to unburden my load
Give a smile, do not shred a tear
As I leave behind the ones I hold dear.

P M Chambers

NOT SO SIMPLE

I thought I'd learn to ride a horse
And so I took a simple course
When to start and when to stop
How to get on and how to get off
But it isn't as easy as it might seem
One day I landed in a stream
We were trotting along quite nice and slow
I thought what a lovely pace to go
Then suddenly the horse neighed and raised his ears
And also raised were my worst fears
He started to gallop with all his might
And though I tried to hold on tight
He went left and I went right
It gave me such a shocking fright
I still have nightmares every night
Although my bumps are very few
I think my horsy days are through.

Vera Lloyd

PROGRESS

In Tamworth I've lived all of my life.
First as a baby, now as a wife.
A childhood spent in countryside,
Peace tranquillity, a certain pride.

Where there was once the quiet road and street,
Erupted the by-pass, now it's just traffic we meet.
In times gone, open your windows and hark,
The hum of the bees, the song of the lark.

Not anymore the countryside sound,
Hear only the traffic noise I'll be bound.
Tamworth has changed, is this progress?
Or does life in our town render distress.

However all is not bad within our town,
Traffic calming slows us all down.
Due to the by-pass, quiet is the A5,
Someone else's life has taken a dive.

We solve our problems day by day
But we pass them on, just give them away.
Increase our roads, the burdens drift,
From one place to another our problems do shift.

Like our coastline eroded and lost,
We suffer from progress, and count the cost.
A country person I'd like to be,
From pollution and traffic let me be free.

Anne Livingstone

CHINKS OF LIGHT...

Darkened windows save lives
So drop the tar and paper blind
Settle down in the firelight
Air raid siren's gone off tonight
The night watchmen walk the streets
Checking windows for any leaks
A baby born by candlelight
Brings new hope in the dead of night
Bakers knead tomorrow's bread
Wives and families in their beds
Trusting when the morning comes
No more bombers... no more guns
Then a chink of light shines across the room
Dawn has broken through the gloom
The all clear siren sounds... the raid subsides
And folk continue with their lives.

Jean Dooley

MY FINAL WORDS

I'd whisper my last words.
Even though they would be full of confusion,
I cannot hear, or see you,
but you still sit and listen carefully to my every word.

I fall deeper and deeper, waiting for you to catch me,
with your arms open wide.

The sun shines, and the birds sing the songs of summer time,
the wind blows through the trees even and cool.

My heart beats slowly as you lay down by my side,
listening to the words I have to say.

You left me just when I needed you most,
but I still love you and I'll always love you.

My heart grows fonder of you more and more each day,
and every second time can count.

It seems like a dream, maybe it's time I should go now,
start a new life and we will meet again,
I know we will never forget those good times 'yes, there were a few'
you remember don't you?

Well the wind is getting stronger, I can feel it blowing across my face,
I cannot see the sun no more maybe, it's gone behind that cloud,

Now I say my final words and they mean so much to us,
I love you and I do care, so much I care,
and maybe one day I will win your heart.

Goodbye my love
Goodbye.

Louise Sandland

THE DISCREET AFFAIR

They went out of town to conduct their affair
Him from the Co-op and her with red hair.
They'd meet in small pubs, holding hands in the dark
And kiss in the bushes in Levenshulme Park.
No-one suspected their sordid affair
Meet in their home town! They just didn't dare.
He'd slice up the hams and dream of her thighs.
She'd grill pork sausage and give a few sighs.

Then came the chance of a week in the sun
Together at last for some sex, sand, and fun!
She told all her family, 'A health farm, for me.'
Sent off for her passport, and then so did he.
He announced to his wife he was going to fish
A week up in Scotland - was always his wish.
So, him from the Co-op and her with red hair
Flew off to Jamaica to have their affair.

Six days and six nights of orgasmic bliss.
He thrilled her plump body and exhausted his.
They staggered downstairs to the bar the last day
And yawned at the view over Montego Bay.

Both went back home - well, he went ahead.
Him to the Co-op - and she went to bed.
Their passions were sated, affair was no more
Till several months later - what came through the door?
The new Travel Brochures - what could we say
That's him and that's her in Montego Bay!
Then everyone knew about the affair
With him from the Co-op and Her with Red Hair!

Enfys Winter

SECOND HAND ROSE

Oh boy! Oh boy! Craft stalls and nearly new,
Oxfam, Cancer Research, to name a few.
Lots of these in every town, and places to eat
the food we oughtna, temptation round every corner,
Jumble sales in such disorder.

Bargains for you and bargains for me,
racks of clothes for you to see.
We rummage around from store to store,
saving money, more and more.

We take them home and give them a wash,
and then we wear them and look all *posh!*

To go to these shops, is a real treat
and in our clothes, we look so neat,
      someone says. . .
      'You look so slim,'
and we just give a knowing grin.

Our Marks and Sparks cost so little,
and yet we look so smart,
I think we've got out shopping spree
off to a fine old art!

It may be something to wear for work,
or perhaps an evening out,
but we're helping ourselves and helping others,
and that's what it's all about.

Janet Hancox

TWO HEARTS

Somewhere in there, there was room for me
Somewhere in there, there was room for two
Somewhere in there, the sun had used to shine
Somewhere in there, was a reserved chamber for me
Somewhere in there, my eyes were always dry
Somehow in there, I had no need to cry.

And now in there, I see a well sealed door
boarded windows,
and not a glimmer of light.
And now in there, I have no private shrine
And now in there
I feel somewhat dislodged.
And now in there,
are broken glass among the pebbles
And then in there
my weakened heart rebel.

Somewhere in here, there is room for you
Somewhere in here, others will be few
Somewhere in here,
your heart will be with mine
and we'll have no need to pine
Somewhere in here, the fire has lost its spark.
No heat, to warm my cooling heart,
Somewhere in there
there is a smouldering
that could re-ignite a flame.

Semba Jallow-Rutherford

THE ENDING

Red rose, lying on the floor,
Deadly, torn apart.
Once a future, a closed door,
Just like a broken work of art.

A tear falls upon a petal,
destroyed, it seems to say.
Stung, as if struck by a nettle.
I yell, wanting it my way.

Why did you leave me?
Alone, deserted, in a place like this.
Why can't you see,
My heart aches for you.

Nigath Bi

UNTITLED

The moon just wants to shine for you
Tis thee that makes the sky so blue,
your face comes in to all my dreams
the sun sees your face and so it beams,
I walk in fields of God made wonder
but of you I'm still much fonder,
with who else, could you I compare
no one! No thing! Does your beauty share,
these are my words of love for you
there are none deeper or more true,
this love we have is so sublime
t'will last until the end of time.

A Felgate

THE KILLING FIELD

The killing fields
Have left their scar
Of life and limb,
They went too far.
The war is over,
Left it's litter,
The common people
Feeling bitter,
The bombs that fell
Like summer rain
Destroyed a country,
All in vain
With heads of state
The generals yield,
The victor is -
The Killing Field.

Roger Barratt

MOTHER

Life grows cold, Dear Mother,
So give me the warmth of your smile.
Rock me and hold me in your arms -
If just for a little while.

Hold me tight, Dear Mother,
Wait for me till I come.
Just an old and feeble dying soul,
But still your little son.

Bernard Ison

WHITE CIDER

Afraid all day, dissatisfied, tremor the hearts of the useless,
But into hero is poverty turned at the hands of trusty white cider.

As glue of the nineties, cheap and so strong, dulls mind of the helpless.
But into a warrior are all fears transformed at the feet of trusty white cider.

A knight in glass armour, giver of strength,
confidence giver to the not needed, abandon the flame of the living. Oh rise omnipresent white cider.

Forget anxiety forsake all fears, your saviour white cider is here is here.
Mind dulled in the evening forget all the pain, when ill in the morning just do it again.

Perplexed with your lot, unwanted terror in the souls of the needy.
But into a monster the tormented change at the beckoning of white cider.

Simmer wrecks of Maggydom.
Forgotten low life created by hands of the greedy. But be content, get out of here with the help of Messiah white cider!

Richard Parkes

CONFUSION

Understanding love requires a higher soul, not mine.
Mysteries of feeling around and around entwine.
Sweet, outrageous, passion, lust, what pleasing words but why?
When misinterpretation bounds and inflamed senses cry
Stop! Peace, now at any cost

Peace to soothe the turmoil, inner-self to sate,
Peace to slow the heartbeats, beating breathless rate.
Peace to combat, reeling senses spinning to relate
How to comprehend the fire?
The Universal glow.
Spontaneous
Outrageous.
Mere mortals cannot know.

These things belong to higher planes,
The spirits comprehend.
So man will fall in love.
Till mortal life shall end
And never understand.

C A Assam

GROW ME STRAWBERRIES

Grow me strawberries, bring me flowers,
Allow me endless hours, of
Soft warm kisses in the dark
Handheld walks in an autumn park.
While running barefoot through fields of red
Let poppy perfume fill our heads.
Deserted beaches we will find
And count the stars in the moonlit sky.
We'll gaze at the waterfall's rainbows made
And wait until their colours fade.
Then step the stones across the lake,
All of Nature's gifts we'll take
To sample, the old and new,
Her beautiful world I'll share with you.

Joy Edmunds

ORPHANED

Oh, Lord shine in
To warm the chilly darkness of a fledgling child,
Plucked at a tender age
From a mother's warm embrace,
The memory of her arms grows dim,
And the beauty of her face.

Cast adrift, Lord,
On the stormy seas of life;
Tossed alongside sibling craft,
There riding unexpected calms
To dream awhile of gentle pools,
Her eyes . . . too soon to wake.

But life goes on.
In force ten gales the fight for breath;
Always searching for the cool, calm breezes
Of a gentler shore.
To lie and feel their soft caress
As a mother's breath upon the cheek,
And roam no more.

Nadine Handy

21 - FULL CIRCLE

How quiet is this house!
No more tiny feet to patter around
No football kit to hunt for till found
The record player (now old fashioned)
Belts out no pop, no jazz, no passion
The rooms are tidy, no need to clean
Nobody uses them, the windows gleam
And all is still.

But wait! A car draws into the drive
Doors slam, a dog barks - they've arrived!
'Granny, Grandad, we're here' they shout
'What's for dinner? Can we go out
to the park - on the roundabout'
Mints, biscuits and cookies they request
Our pantry and patience are put to the test
It's pandemonium!

It's time to go
Dinner and tea, all they could eat
To be bathed at Granny's - a special treat
Play with the ducks who squirt water all ways
Shrieks of laughter, what happy days
The car is packed, cakes to take home
Hugs and kisses and then they are gone.
How quiet is this house!

Dorothy Ripley

THE LEGACY

You see them stand on corners cold
Hearts still young but spirits old
Acting tough and talking loud
Trying hard to fit the crowd
Talking up their desperate dreams
While clinging to their self esteem
They have no heroes only peers
Who share a smoke and buy the beers
They are a generation lost
Their future is to count the cost
And market forces set the price
And theirs will be the sacrifice

Harry Smith

UNTITLED

Should I write some poetry?
Should I make it rhyme?
Will it be of bygone days
Or about this present time?
Will it be a sonnet, or an ode unto the spring?
Or shall I praise the nightingale
or a swallow on the wing?
It seems I'm in a quandary
I'm puzzled what to write
Shall it be of morning, or an ode unto the night?
So many things to think about
In this magic world of ours
Of trees and birds, and butterflies
Of green grass and of flowers
So I'll just be thankful
I've mentioned quite a few
And count my blessings every day
With thanks dear Lord to you.

Florence Carvell

A NOT SO HAPPY ENDING

They tuck me in and say 'Goodnight,
Sleep tight; don't let the bedbugs bite.'
As if I'd be afraid of those,
Who have to hide beneath bedclothes.
So then I'm all alone in bed,
With parable-magic in my head.

Princesses wail to handsome knights,
As archers nobly aim in tights.
The castle stands a bookcase tall,
As plants climb up the stony wall.
A dragon lurks beneath the bed;
I cuddle Tuck, my bravest Ted.

Prince Sam rides out of Fairy Land.
He sees the castle fall when rammed.
King 'Snap-a-lot' now wants his head.
The princess found is almost dead.
The magic they cannot defend.
And that, my friends, they call *the end*.

Yvonne Harrison

AN AWAKENING FLOWER

With a brisk breeze blowing
With each individual petal gently.
Unfolding.
Reaching out but all that is there, is
the refreshing air.
A fragrant smell lingered around, and then
a sudden sound, came from the
ground.
A wide open space.
A secret place.
Something colourful, beautiful and
new.
Alive for without you to care for
me.
I'd dry, wilt, and eventually
die.

A Scott

COME OUTSIDE

When all your days seem empty
      when darkness falls too soon
Don't hide away with memories
      inside your empty room
Do come outside
      and look around
There's so much you can do
      for someone, not so far away
May need a friend like you
      you're missing all the treasures
That God has given all
      the air we breathe
The sun the rain
      all creatures great and small.
The country and its scenery
      and flowers in all their splendour
A tiny child may look and smile
      their hearts are warm and tender
Don't let your days seem empty
      don't hide behind your gloom
Do come outside and join us
      There's love, there's warmth, there's room.

Margaret Ensor

EXTRA CURRICULUM ACTIVITY

The bell chimed four, and I was out that
door as fast as I could be.
I was on the bus, no pushing, no fuss
And home for four-thirty.

I'll ignore my homework in my bag,
Copy it down from a pal in the morning
(Mam doesn't know I've done that before,
And I'm on a final warning).

But I'll risk detention, I don't care,
Yes, homework can definitely wait,
'Cos the most gorgeous boy from the
upper sixth,
Has tonight asked me out for a date.

Josephine Burnett

RAIN IS FREE

Standing at the window,
Looking at the rain,
All that lovely water,
Rushing down the drain.

Will it swell the rivers,
Flooding fields and streams,
Causing countless damage,
Dashing many dreams.

Or will it be collected,
And purified to drink,
Far more beneficial,
Any one would think.

One thing is for certain,
No matter whichever way,
It'll increase the water rates,
That I have to pay.

Jack Snape

SPARE OUR CHILDREN

The smiling faces, sounds of glee,
to see them playing, so happily.
But spare a thought, for those who are sad,
who have nothing but terror, in a life so bad
Innocent victims, of plagues and wars,
they are the sufferers, and not the cause.
In Africa, where famine and aids, take their toll,
where innocent children, have no control.
In Asia, where child labour, and prostitution are rife,
do these children, deserve such a life?
In Europe, where perverts prey, on those so young,
children made to feel, they are the ones doing wrong.
In America, where it is easy, to get drugs or a gun,
a child's life too serious, when it should be fun.
When marriages break up, followed by divorce,
it is the children who suffer, they feel they are the cause.
Our children's happiness, we should not steal,
we should be aware, of just how they feel.
As adults we deny, our children their rights,
we make them suffer, through all of our fights.
Take care of the children, for they are our tomorrow,
we should give them happiness, and not so much sorrow.
It is not a crime, for them to laugh and shout,
we should not get angry, and order them out.
Out into streets, where it is no longer safe to play,
we should listen, to what our children say.
We can learn a lot, from a child's innocence,
how they see life, makes a lot more sense.
They do not wage war, or destroy the earth,
it is a real pleasure, to see them so full of mirth.

Stephen McGowan

THE STUFF THAT DREAMS ARE MADE OF

She sat on a stagecoach,
I sat on the roof of our old shed,
She rode a Palomeno,
I rode mum's old bike instead.
She wore buckskin trousers,
And I wore faded jeans,
But me and Calamity Jane, we were the 50's cow-girl queens.

She had a Winchester rifle,
A broken bean-stick that was mine.
She had reins of leather,
I had a washing line.
She shot lots of Indians, and loved Bill Hickcock, so they say,
I shot dad's old chickens, and I loved Doris Day.

She was a great big movie star,
And I was just a kid.
But I loved everything about her,
And everything she did.
That was 40 years ago,
And now I'm old and grey,
But I'm still the biggest fan there is
Of a star called Doris Day.

If I get that winning Lottery ticket,
I'm off to the USA.
I'm going to see if I can find
That star called Doris Day.
I'll hang around her supermarket,
And you know, if I'm in luck,
I'll walk right up to her and say
'Can I push your trolley duck?'

Angela Green

UNTITLED

I had a dog I knew quite well
until one day he went and fell
I took him home and laid him down
and covered him with my dressing gown

Morning came, so I went to see
just how well my dog would be
what greeted me was quite a shock
he'd upped and gone, and knicked the clock

I called the cops they'd help me look
for this clever, canine crook
he'd have to pay for this foul deed
the trouble was we had no lead

Time went by the case was closed
of the clock no-one knows
and what became of that fiendish hound
he probably landed in the pound

The moral of this tale you've read
don't leave the clock when you go to bed
'cos if you do, he'll go deceive ya
that sleeping dog, that old retriever.

Damian Carter

DAY'S END

Sunset deeps, with fading ochre ray,
Full soon to end the autumn day:
Exhaled sweet breath, of evening chill.
Crisping grass and herbs on darkening hill.
Whispers soft, with curious misty glee,
Ruffles spans of curling fern, and tall pine tree
Silent now, with hooded eye, the erstwhile strident jay.

Dark herald of night descends: with spreading cloak
To blur the branches of the twisted oak
To creep in secret stealth to blend
With grey hued garb, sweet earth and fissured clay.
The childish flowers, the hollows of decay.
All is muted, still, entranced with strange delight
To welcome, hushed, the calm serenity of night.

F G Sutton

SUNNY HOLLOW LAGOON

Wind filled sails to distant lands
Love filled hearts in tender hands,
Gently carried beneath the new moon
Destination for lovers, Sunny Hollow Lagoon.

Canvas and rigging taking the strain
Journey of romance there to remain,
Wrapped within a cloak of love
Hearts at sea floating blithely above.

Fervent hearts on voyage of desire
Indulgence of lovers one to inspire,
Tailwind blowing as from the start
Consideration as though it has heart.

Guiding star with your effulgent light
Enkindler of love's flame at night,
Show the island of lovers' dreams
With the moon direct your beams.

By the island sails at rest
A dream fulfilled an haven blest,
A special star, a special moon
Home for lovers, Sunny Hollow Lagoon.

Peter James O'Rourke

UNTITLED

One more glance up and along this low lit street,
A glance, now bored, so many times do I repeat.
To look extraordinary, quite misplaced, one of the crowd,
For my standing here looking, gazing, awaiting is not allowed.
I am what some call, in less lurid tones 'Lady of the Night'
Others call me 'hooker' or 'pro', but they don't sound at all polite.
My feelings to what they say or even what they do,
Have long since vanished, as do summer skies of blue.
No leafy lanes on balmy nights do I 'A pleasant walk',
Or with a lover, hand in hand, whispering small talk.
My conversations are course, abrupt, don't beat about the bush,
Replies sometimes stammered, with ducked head said ne'er cause a blush.
And so once more up and along the low lit street I glance,
A city gent, a husband so misunderstood, a youth taking his first chance.
This lurid task that I perform, no harm wished toward anyone,
Will still be here, upon some low lit street, although I shall be gone.
Don't curse at me, call 'slut' or cow upon the pill,
For beneath this sham, I have a life, a dream within me still.

D McDonald

ANNIVERSARY

Where is yesterday - forever gone like melting snow,
Where is tomorrow - forever out of reach in spite of all we know
Where is today - forever here and now like a fleeting sound
With yesterday and tomorrow all around
And, so my love, as each today is done
We share our memories of yesterday
And our dreams for tomorrow yet to come.

Charles Todd

BROKEN MEMORIES

Take a child and put in care
Will that child be happy there
Or will that smile hide tears of fear

Good people you must learn to see
Deep within this child so still
What they will find
And cannot see
They took away my family
I do not know I do not care
I don't want to be taken there.

I find this strange
Why don't they shout
I've spilt my milk, I'll get a clout
What is this, it's time to play
These toys are mine they say

Time for bed I feel so scared
No-one but me in this big bed
To hold on tight, my ears will strain
To hear someone fighting once again

No noise - so quiet
Just someone saying
You all right?
So warm, so safe,
I guess this is a lovely place.

Bea Evans

THE SEA

O, mighty sea that pounds the rocks,
That claws at land and tries,
To vent its wrath on lonely cliffs,
Screaming at silent skies,
For when you storm your roaring voice,
We cannot bear to hear,
The power that drives you from above,
Makes humans cringe, with fear,
The men that venture on your waves,
Are species of a kind, they trust, they know,
That all in all, you are the master mind,
Their fate, they know, lies in your choice,
But be with you they must,
To gratify the unknown urge, and stay, within your clutch,
The treasures you have guarded long,
Are theirs to come and take,
Your anger or resentment, will no difference make,
They'll dig beneath your mighty shelf,
For liquid gold, and untold wealth,
Harness you, they never can,
But they do not give a damn,
Life you give, and life you take,
All mankind makes this mistake.

Edna Hunt

MY LOVE

When I put my head on my pillow
My thoughts are all of you,
Your laughing face, your loving arms
The thoughtful things you do.

You've made my empty life complete
My grey skies now are blue,
My step is light, in my eyes a smile
Because of knowing you.

Oh that we could be as one
And start our lives anew,
But you are bound by bands of gold
That cannot be cut through.

So count the days till we meet again,
Think of me as I think of you,
Till our lips touch and arms entwine
And dreams perchance come true.

Amy Willetts

WHICH

Are you a homemaker or do you just keep house?
Do you always cook a tasty meal for your beloved spouse?
Do you skip thro' the household chores or do they get you down?
Do you visit friends in hospital to help pass the dreary day,
Or are you mean and selfish and like having your own way?
Do you turn sheets side to middle when you find they're wearing thin?
Do you mend and make do cheerfully or just throw things in the bin?
Life can be so much easier if you put on a brave face,
So spread happiness around and make the world a better place!

K M Hewitt

TIME

As I listen to the clock ticking on the wall,
And watch the leaves change colour and wither as they fall.

As I witness a child change daily as soon as he is born,
And perceive the inevitable yield of night to morn.

As I gaze upon the ocean surging to and from the shore,
And feel the clement season give way to Winter's war.

I'm filled with insignificance, humbleness and awe.

Patricia Jamieson

THE FIREBIRD

When the dawn creeps into light,
Shakes off its shroud of darkened night,
The Firebird ascends, begins its flight,
Spreads its wings of glowing light.

It rises slowly to the sky,
Leading shadows as it flys,
Sailing over without a cry,
Silently it passes by.

When dusk falls, without a sound
The Firebird dips towards the ground,
It lights the sky all around,
And the horizon, with beauty's crowned.

Debra Davis

HAPPY'S REFLECTION

My sister had a budgie
An easy bird to rear,
He wasn't any trouble,
And filled the house with cheer.

My sister thought that somehow
She'd teach the bird to speak,
But all she ever heard,
Was squeak, squeak, squeak.

My sister bought a mirror
And put it in the cage,
But when the budgie saw it,
Thought he was on the stage.

Now Happy had a partner
And did a double act,
He never learned to talk to us,
Because he had a pact.

M Brassington

MY DADDY

To have a daddy is one good thing,
To have you daddy is everything
I know you're very proud of me,
I hope that you will always be,
I love you daddy very much,
When to your big strong arms I clutch
It's then I feel quite safe and sound
Because I know that you are around.

A Fullbrook (11)

A CHILD ALONE

I'm a child alone, a child afraid.
In a time of crisis man has made.
I'm an orphan, a refugee alone in my land.
My future destroyed by the gun in his hand.

Ravaged by war my country is lost.
My home life destroyed at a terrible cost.
My dreams have all faded my hopes are no more.
I'm a child of the time, a child of a war.

I'm a child of depression, a child filled with pain.
My mother and father I won't see again.
My brother and sisters are lost in this land.
Why is this happening I don't understand.

My face will haunt them in years to come.
These men who carelessly carry a gun.
I hope they will find a way for their hatred to cease.
Perhaps the child of tomorrow will then live in peace.

Josephine Banks

MY BENJI

Loving friend you will always be
From now until Eternity.
Those big brown eyes and loving ways,
Will linger with me for always.

We go for walks each day together
Along the lane despite the weather,
You will have a good dig, chase the birds,
You are far to funny for words.

I love you so much, I wish we never have to part,
Because a part of you is always in my heart,
Death comes to us all I am very sad to say,
God is good so we have to live from day to day.

May Ward

SON

The prettiest child I've ever seen
and you belonged to me
a chubby face
with eyes so blue
your rosy cheeks
and hair so white
you really was a lovely sight

We brought you home
We loved you so
I wanted all the world to know
that I'd brought home
my pride and joy
my darling sweetheart
little boy

Now years have flown
and you have grown
a son we can be proud of
the years may come
the years may go
but still our love
for you will grow.

Carol Davies

SCORN ME NOT

Scorn me not as you pass by
I am that friendly shade beneath the sky
I screen you from the noon day sun
In winter's storms I warm you when your daily toil is done
My fruits shall quench your longing thirst
My arms support your thatch
My trunk shall be your table
Your casement and your sash
I am your tools of trade, without them you are lost
I am the bed where in you lie, the cradle where you rock.
Your cot from me created with tender loving care
And I shall be your coffin when you are lying there
The door of this your homestead was fashioned out of me
Then scorn me not as you pass by, for I am just a tree.

Norman Hancock

TO MY FELLOW DREAMERS

As I lie here enveloped by the warm
golden fingers of the sun,
I dream and wait for a day which
has not yet begun.

A day when all my hopes and ambitions
can be fulfilled,
All those sniggers and doubts killed.

A day when I stand out from the
crowd,
When for once I can be proud.

There's so much of the world that I
want to see,
But who holds that golden key?

Is it God or is it fate?
One thing I know, it's never too late.
If you feel defeated and in despair,
Don't just sit back in your chair.

But take heed, some hope, some
hard work and a little ambition,
that's all you need.

Fiona Tuckwell

PATIENCE

My heart in fragments lies this day
Because of you; yet only you
Can show the way
To live again. But will life be so sweet?
Can love, once hurt, return again complete?

Why should you seek to hurt me so?
I wait for one sweet uttered word
From you, for you must know
You are my world. And yet as time goes past,
I whisper to myself, 'Will this love last?'

But loving hearts, on tender wings
Will let time pass, while waiting silently.
For sweeter things.
For your return. Yes, now I know you will,
My heart, no more in fragments, loves you still.

Marie P Holbeche

MY IMMORTAL BEING

I'm not famous,
Or even well known,
I'm just me,
Me alone,
But, remember me when I am gone,
For within my children; I'll live on,
Flesh of my flesh,
They'll hold my knowledge,
Memories happy, sad, good and bad,
They are of me,
My meaning,
My immortal being

Tracey Wiggins

MOTHER

Your blue eyes never could trust anyone.
Suspiciously they interrogate
Fixing visitor's friendly gaze
in accusatory stare.

Don't want none - whatever it is.
Not today thank you.
Too nervous to allow enquiry
Hands twitch in defence mode.

You'd like us to believe you're stone.
We negotiate sharp edges
but everything about you cries out
for someone to believe in you.

A lifetime of emotion compressed
Into a small hollow heart
Too painful to acknowledge.
You live behind an eggshell mask.

You are inside the unloved child
Whose brother bullied, whose sister died.
Are you too old to forgive
and live with who you are?

Jan Eyton

UNTITLED

Why does reason fail me now?
That I should find myself in hell
That nature takes the breast from me
That I must turn to you.

Why does rich me seek unnatural things?
To hide the pain of life behind
The unfortunate brace which knowledge brings
And I will turn to you.

Why can't they understand my needs?
That always I am left alone
With only time preventing me from finding peace
That I shall turn to you.

Why does distance separate us?
Yet thoughts suggest that you are close
And closing eyes I see your face
And I will be with you.

D Stych

SEASONS

I love the feel of the seasons,
The magic of change in the air,
Just as we think we are in winter's gloom
A tiny white snowdrop, bursts into bloom.
It seems to say, it won't be long now,
Before golden daffodils take a bow.
The trees reach out, dressed in spring attire,
Fresh and green, and full of power.
The soft winds whisper, and gently blow.
The air is warm now, in summer's glow.
But all too soon, the glory will fade.
There's stillness now, in wood and glade.
But oh what splendour, all around.
Fountains of gold, in woods abound.
Through the mists, the miracle is lost.
The chill now feel of November frost
Bites at earth, and seems to say,
Dark December is here to stay.
But when we see the sky aglow,
Even this will change we know.
Oh, what blessings each day we see,
They cost us nothing, they all are free.

D Fellows

BELIEFS

If in God we do believe
The Garden of Eden and Adam and Eve
Then it follows it must be true
That there is a Devil too
So if in Heaven you wish to dwell
Do good on Earth or end up in Hell

A L Price

WHO CARES?

I needed to explain, but who cares?
You don't, any more than the next.
I wanted to be different.
Not like you or anyone else
Just my own person
Doing my own thing
Thinking my own thing
But who cares?

In the end I gave up
I can't expect anyone else to listen
Not any more, not now
Maybe not ever
I'm now like everyone else
But who cares?

My thoughts are jumbled into one,
The way I think,
The way you think,
And the way everyone else thinks
What I am, is not me
Not the real me
Just the me everyone wants me to be.
But who cares?

What I'd always wanted to say
Needn't be said, not anymore
It's too late
I'm not me anymore
I'm you and you and you all mixed up
But who cares?

S A Clay

ELEPHANTS

Elephants persist, at the top of the list, of the mammals known best,
                                        it is true;
But, there are facts that exist, that you may have missed, that are
                                        known to only a few:
The way they evolved is strangely involved with the hyrax, of all things,
                                        it's stated;
'They say now, that the dugong and Sea-cow, were at one time with
                                        elephants related.
The extinct mastodon and the mammoth, now gone, were the modern
                                        elephants' kin;
And, the word 'pachyderm' is an Ancient Greek term for the elephant's
                                        very thick skin.
They eat kilos a day of grass, shrubs and hay; and are the largest of
                                        mammals land-bound.
And, interest increases to find two different species 'twixt which wide
                                        variations are found:
One comes from Africa and have very large ears, which are rather fan-like
                                        in shape;
Its tusks, it appears, are large like its ears; it lives from Sudan to the Cape.
The other, from Asia, stands not so tall, its ears are smaller and firmer;
The tusks are quite small, some have none at all; it's found in Sri Lanka
                                        and India to Burma.
Now, the naturalist Linneaus, with a masterly stroke, classified all living
                                        things in a pattern,
So that no matter what folk, or the language they spoke, could identify
                                        all in the Latin:
Loxodonta Africana, for instance, you'll find is the Latin for African
                                        Elephant;
And the Latin defined for the Asian kind *Elephas maximus* is the
                                        name that is relevant.

So it is not so absurd to find Latin preferred to explain in a form very neat,
That *plantigrade* is the word that is usually heard to explain that 'they walk
                                                on the soles of their feet.'
Here's another strange fact that few of us know, how the species differ,
                                  yet again, from each other
The African type grows a less number of toes than its smaller Asian brother.
On the African elephant's feet you will find - four toes on the front ones
                                  and three behind;
The Asian one differs by having one more: four toes at the rear and
                                  five at the fore!
At the tips of their trunks, which they use as a hose, there is a prehensile,
                                  sensitive member;
Where only one grows on the Asian one's nose, the African has two -
                                  please remember!

They have one thing in common the observer sees, you must watch how
                                  they walk to view it:
Just like us, if you please, their hind legs bend at the knees; they're the only
                                  four-legged mammal to do it!
The tusks that they wear are their downfall I fear, they give them the ugly
                                  distinction
Of joining the list of those doomed to exist with the threat if impending
                                  extinction.
The slaughter is caused by the ivory trade, for which there is simply no need.
This primitive trade is a curse that is made by superstition, cruelty and greed.
So, poachers, take care, there's no future for you, nor the traders who give
                                  you your bread;
Now that the World is aware of your evil, *Beware*; it's not the elephants
                                  we want to see dead.

Ray Hutchins

YOU ARE MINE

The hand to grip
and talk out loud
the eyes that smile
and skin that knows.

A rush of love
an instant lock
with a river to flow
and a sun to shine
You are mine
'Forever Divine'

Leoni Williams

WHAT IS IT FOR?

The sun and moon
they sit so high
to view the likes of you and I.
Upon the earth
a fiery mass
where man is born
to slowly die.

Merely man
they're born so small
they grow to nothing big or tall.
Quite unique
in many ways
their life to them
is one and all.

In fact a hint of life
a tiny race
a speck of dust in infinite space.
In such vast expanse
there must be more
what is its end?
What is it for?

Philip Carter

COTSWOLD INTERLUDE

The urgent voices from another world
Slip into silence here, where stone walls dream
By poppied fields; where ferns lie cool and curled
Asleep beside the prattle of a stream.
No need for quick decision stirs the brain
To match with anxious beat the pulse of time.
This narrow, idle, winding little lane
Goes rambling through all restlessness of mine.
Somewhere a city street exacts its due
Of grime and weariness - once there again
Shall I recall how honeysuckle grew
In tangled, creamy clusters? How the flame
Of vagrant rose, setting a hedge alight,
Kindled my heart to sudden swift delight?

Winifred Mustoe

CHRIS AND JOHN'S HONEY

John and I went shopping to buy a brand new pet
We went down to the kennels to see what we could get
Something with a pedigree we thought would do just fine
We went across the compound, started walking down the line.

We saw so many puppies, it was really hard to choose
Some were sitting on their own, some sat there in two's
And then we spotted Honey and said, 'she's the one for us.'
We paid a sum of money and gave her lots of fuss.

Now John and I have got her home, she really is a treat
That's why we called her Honey, because she is so sweet.

Jean Skitrall

IF I SHOULD DIE

Day one -

How heavy things seem today
Such that there is little compensation
For this distorted beat replaces reason

I walk a little faster
Or a little further according to dictation
And find myself outside of the hypothesis of life

The weight of a limb
Hidden by diurnal motion
Strikes within my mind against a chord

Day two -

If I should die, then I shall die
For who am I to protest
And out of body I observe the scene

Rest assured I shall return
With thoughts aroused and symptoms read
Like lines upon the body tell a tale

All around my feet they stand
Upon their faces I see but false grief
For all believe that this was for the best.

P C Walker

CULTURE IN THE SKY

When this town starts to get me down
The noise of the traffic all around
I just lift my eyes to the sky
And I can fly into the skyline

There's so many shapes to see
Attics point inspiringly
Turrets tower with pigeon power
And I can float away

The bears on the 'Bear Hotel'
The lions above the 'Windsor'
Look down on this zoo of hell
As humans rush to buy and sell

It seems our culture's in the sky
But who can see such grace
Swept along in today's rat race
The style of an age gone by

Barbara Ann Betts

UNTITLED

Come hither ye all and harken to my tale
It is the saga of one who was doomed to fail
Although kind of heart and spirit so strong
Every act he performed always seemed to go wrong
Through no fault of his own his misfortune increased
His stricken body and mind were never at peace
Until one day he came upon a wizened old man
Who looked exhausted and almost at the end of his span
A thought crossed his mind, there am I of the future
If his luck is as mine his life has been torture
I will ease his load and if only for a day
He will find relief that will help him on his way
This he did and with an encouraging smile
Assisted the old man for many a mile
The God's looking down all noticed this act
Decided to change his fortune, and it is now a known fact
That he prospered and gained all the good things in life
Through taking the trouble to help another in strife.

D Beecroft

INTO STARDOM

All the sharing and caring
has been wearing me down
to a thin, little shadow
of my old fifteen stone.

All the seeing to you
all the being with you;
your wants and needs
down to pulling up your weeds -

well, I've lost six stone
in just over a year,
and the time has come
yes it has, my dear -

to break the big tidings. . .
I'm off to the States,
first to go on 'Oprah'
to spill about my weight.

For my book's in the
best seller lists and
the root of my success
is due to you my dear
and your d*** laziness.

Alyson Faye

SEEING

Why is it when we're feeling sad
The only things we see seem bad?
We only notice dirt and mud,
We miss the things that looked so good
When we were feeling bright.

Do we need pills to paint things blue
When they look grey? No, that's not true,
A little child can give us eyes
To see the pictures in the skies
And put the world to right.

He'll see the golds, not just the brown
Of leaves left scattered on the ground.
The vision of a child is great,
If only *we'd* not learned to hate
The world would look all right.

Sandra Holden

SUPERSTARMUM

What can I say about our mum,
Only that she has a big bum,
Shirley Bassey is a very big star
but no bigger star than my ma.
Living and giving is her best thing,
All four of us, we all bring
lots of grandchildren to make her happy,
Even Emily's smelly nappies - Sayings!
      'Where's my beautiful baby
      Sophie is a little lady
      Now Chelsey will be better when she's 10
      and Harry's micky will stop soon - when?
      And Shelly's growing up - a little Missus Muck
      Matty is a lovely lad, plays football with no luck
Drinking Brandy from a glass with a very wide brim
Just so that she can get her nose in
At all our parties and do's, she's the ace card
And when she swears, she's in the farmyard
Everyone knows about the pies she says she's made herself.
Also she's the pretty one, looks better from round-a-bout.
She's wonderful and a really good friend
Though sometimes she shouts and my ear bends
Always there in times of need
giving us advice and notices to heed
I could go on about you mum forever more
And just how much you are adored
this is just to tell you we love you lots
from all of us and our tiny tots.

P Summerscales

BEDD TALIESIN - SUMMER 1995

Solemn lay the stone, a barren rock in a barren land,
Grey and grizzled, clad with moss and ferns
And seeming like the many rocks the strewed the
Sheep-shorn slope. There was no outward show,
Naught to reveal how well the rock had kept its troth
And guarded through a thousand years the fragile bones beneath.

For here, abandoned in his native soil, lies one
Whose name burnt bright throughout the land,
Who wove his magic in the elder days
When Arthur and his queen sat on the throne
And warrior chiefs held sway beneath the king:
When the Saxon bayed, impatient, at the gate.

Who was this man? Who knows his true life's tale?
Another Merlin weaving magic webs,
A prophet piercing time's mysterious veil
To reveal the stormy future of his land?
Or a simple bard who sung such tales of yore
That all who heard him fell beneath his spell?

We know not, but that he was great,
A leader of his land in troubled times,
A name nigh worshipped long after he had gone,
His memory kept by a people still his own -
The name of Taliesin rings through time,
The greatest bard to breathe God's holy air.

And still his spirit lingers in the song
And voice and nature of his land,
Yet here, beneath this cold and barren rock,
Moulding, forgotten, lie his last remains,
And no-one comes to cheer his lonely sleep,
Or voice a prayer for the comfort of his soul.

Susan M Bullock

WINTER

Winter is coming to my door,
With chilling breath and frozen claw,
She wraps the world in her icy mane,
Until the spring should come again,
Her icicles hang long and thin,
Her friend Jack Frost pricks our skin.

Outside we see that it is snowing,
So winter sets a gale blowing,
Soon there is a cold snow storm,
But in this house it's snug and warm
We pity those left out this night,
To suffer winter's numbing bite.

Winter freezes waters deep,
She sends animals to dreamless sleep,
Her foggy breath spreads all around,
Her snowy footsteps mark the ground,
Winter has an evil grin,
So shut the door and don't let her in.

When winter decides it's time to go,
She gathers up her trail of snow,
Jack Frost gently takes her hand
And step by step they leave the land,
Animals wake and plants regrow,
Freed from the chilling layer of snow.

Adam Henderson

MARCH WIND AND SUMMER SUN

The old March wind and summer sun
Argued who was the stronger one
Of course it's I, the wind did say
But summer sun did tell him, nay.

Now from a hut a man appeared
With long grey coat and shaggy beard
The wind said, 'Now here's what we'll do
To see who's stronger of the two.'

The one to make that man divest
His coat and show his manly chest
Shall be proclaimed the winner, so
and summer sun just said 'Right-O.'

Now old March wind did puff and blow
With rain and sleet and flakes of snow
But from the man there came no sound
Just pulled his coat more tightly round.

With old March wind's strong final whine
The summer sun was all benign
The man has not removed his coat
So let me try, though I'll not gloat.

Now summer sun became quite hot
The bearded one untied the knot
That held his coat, then mopped his face
And looked around for cooler place.

He then took off his coat and made
A beeline for the trees and shade
And so, my friends, I say to you
Who was the stronger of the two.

William Littleford

PANDORA DRIVING

They come up like strings of diamonds,
the cats' eyes,
and we add our rubies and our opals,
setting them in kaleidoscope clusters
against the black silk lining
- black, shot with orange and grey -
of this jewel box
where the motorway is caught.
Cut velvet trees along the verges
alternate with flat studs of sapphire
that point to where
other rhinestone delights
stab the soft dark spaces.
Sometimes chunks of amber
fly by, embedded in barbaric findings
of heavy metal
whose colour fades into the shot silk.
Above it all
the pendant moon swings,
a great pearl set in the distant lid.

Jane Moreton

THE WORKING MAN

The hive of industry moves on,
Man does his daily chores,
Wednesday goes, his coupon done,
Saturday see the scores.

He hopes one day to match the two,
His shackles to unchain,
Until he does - I'm sure of this,
It's back to work again

Like Robert Bruce he'll try again,
Endeavouring to succeed,
Can this be human nature?
Or is it really greed.

Whichever is the answer,
Whate'er a man has got,
He'll simply go on trying,
To improve his blooming lot.

Tom Grocott

DIFFERENCES

The snow lies gently on the hills
With snowdrops shining through
Such precious gentle little flowers.
But why are there so few.
When yellow carpets stretch around
of daffodils galore
The difference is between the sea
and sandy sloping shores
and people too can be the same
the quiet and gentle kind.
Then the big and strong
With loud and forceful minds,
With elephants and kangaroos
Mice and little ants
Storms and rain
and burning sun
that really makes us pant.
How mother nature sets us all
upon an even keel,
and when you look around. Each day
it gives you quite a feel.

J Watson

LIFE'S LIKE A THIN GOLDEN THREAD

Life's like a thin golden thread,
Watch the steps with which you tread.
Some glisten and glow at the rim,
Some fade, look shabby and dim.
Yet they're hardened deeply trod,
The painful ones sharply prod.
But gently also imbedded thin,
A golden happiness held within.
So watch each foot as it hits the ground,
What rings out within it's sound.
There your future calmly lies,
Stepping out with its deathly cries.

Susan Rimmer

KNOWHERE

I am here and you are there
Is there something I should know
Here is something you should be aware of
There is somewhere that is not here
And here is somewhere that is not there
Perhaps, if you could be here and I there
then we would both know where,
We are neither here nor there,
For that which is here to me is there to you
and here to you is there to me
I just want to know why I'm there -
                        don't you?

Shane Glasby

EMPTY HOME

Just empty rooms
This house we once called home
Just bricks and mortar now
How I'm missing you
Raindrops falling down the windows
Where you used to stand
Maybe they are crying too

The summer breeze has lost its warmth
The whispering trees seem ill at ease
The patio where you'd sit, you loved the view
A cool chill as the evening falls
Shadows climb around the walls
Just emptiness, how I'm missing you.

The old log fire
On the Persian rug where we'd lie outstretched
Two bodies joined as one
No sense of time
Just loving, giving pleasure until morning light
No more pleasure now you've gone.

Street lights shining through the curtains
On the crystal vase left on the shelf
A rainbow of colours
How I wish that you could see
You loved the simplest things
Warm summer nights, our walks in spring
This empty house
Too many memories here for me.

Judith Brimble

CREATION BY THE CREATOR

With persistent thought and imagination
God silently worked to plan creation
From an infinite volume of darkness and space
He decided to build a visible place
A universe of size beyond question
With time introduced as a fourth dimension
Then from the darkness he made light
It was the work of a genius and a vision for sight
Planets of mass he then positioned in space
One being for animals and a human race
Weather was then added, wind, sunshine, snow and rain
With rivers, plants and seas, to cover all the terrain
Next came air and temperature, with food and water in part
So he now had the vital ingredients for all the living to start
He then made all the creatures with life given at birth
To commence the living and dying upon his planet earth
How long this will keep recurring
Us mere humans can only guess
But certainly the chances of knowing
May be getting less and less.

E Wentworth

THE STRAY

She lived in the house on the corner,
But they moved and left her behind.
The new people had a dog and didn't want her.
Still she stayed, it was home in her mind.

When we realised, all the neighbours and us,
Unknown to each other we bought tins
And put down saucers of milk, made a fuss
Of that skinny little mite, oh so thin.

Holidays came and we went away,
Worried for two weeks that she'd starve.
With no-one to feed her all day
When we got back would she still be alive?

Turned out that while we were gone
Every house in the street fed that brat
And whilst we were worrying and wan
She'd turned into the biggest *fat cat!*

Sandra Kozian

THE WIND

The wind blows in o'er the waves of the sea
Fresh and salt and clean.
Its sharp breath drubs upon my skin.
It scours and sears my aching lungs
And drums in my ears and deafens me
With its shrieks and gusty roar.
It throbs around in my weary head
Cleansing each fibre of my being.
It blasts away the city's dust,
And is sweeter far than the traffic's din.
Not harsh nor grating in discord,
Bringing ease to my troubled mind,
As I walk alone by the water's edge,
Crunching the pebbles on the deserted shore.

Margaret Westwell

I'M NEXT DOOR

I was interested to see what e' was doing next door,
So I picked up the sheets off bed I'd just thrown on floor,
Opened the window - wide - and draped 'em artistically over the sill,
For airing. That's my excuse and I'm stickin' to it still.
Just then that big spotted dog from t'other side started to bark,
'Cum up 'ere our Carol,' I said 'and see this for a lark,
It'll be an education for you, you won't forget
On what not to marry when your turn comes pet,
What on earth do you think 'e's doing then - yon' Fred?'
'Oh Mother! Mabel next door says he's erecting a shed.'
'Are you sure duck? It looks more like a badly constructed bonfire,
I could be wrong though - mind you that Mabel's a little liar,'
Well I mean look at it from 'ere as a whole it's a right old tangle.
If it's a shed why's that side shaped like a triangle?'
'That side' as you call it is part of the roof mother,
He's resting it on the ground and holding it up with the other.'
'Well that '*other*' as you call it has just gone over giving his big 'ead
                                                          a big clout.'
'Get back in mother and close window afore you fall out.'
'Hey Carol, somethin' covered in grime is emerging from the rubble,
Great fool, I tell you straight, steer clear, he spells disaster and trouble.'
It was then that Fred from next door looked up, I could see he was all
                                                        of a fluster,
He said, 'If you don't want them rags on t'sill to blow about missus, I'll
                                                      'ave one for a duster.'
I thought, 'that does it, enough's enough, slammed down window and
                                                    fumbled to lock it,
While one sheet sailed towards spotty dog, and pole with my best flowered
                                    curtains on came right out its socket.

Laura McNeeney

DILATION

a thin wind swept across the board
that chequered floor
where pawns and their pornographers meet
and swarm in chemical deadlock
when out of the blue you appeared
for an instant
ecstatic
spinning in the chaos with your eyes shut

a halo of late
twentieth century light
sainted you in the otherwise darkness
your entire body
a storm of streamlined movement

you were high on something I think
I thought I must be in heaven
or in love or somewhere
else

but on reflection
I think I
unaccustomed to such near perfection
must have been hallucinating
joining dots around the edges
of things that have no edges

because if not
if these things took place anywhere
other than here
on this saltstreaked sheet of A4
then my life's work is complete
ahead of schedule
and I can sleep now.

Nick Staines

CRACK

Eighteen years old girl, living in a box,
It's got no door, it's got no locks.
Her good looks ravaged by the drug they call crack.
One more life fucked, there's no going back.
Selling her body for ten lousy quid,
Thinking of life when she was just a kid;
Happy smiling faces - it's all just a blur,
The feeling of joy so precious and rare:
Just skin and bones she ain't eaten in days,
One more rock and life's just a haze;
One more life just lost on the street,
Uncared for, unloved and well and truly beat.
What's happened to this world of ours,
With all the fat, rich people in their ivory towers;
Looking down on the crap that we call life,
Oblivious to the pain, hurt, trouble and strife.
One more life that will be snuffed out soon,
A soul as lonely as the waning moon.
Those poor forgotten people that time passes by,
Not giving shit if they live or die;
One day maybe, life will be sweet,
For the sad tragic people who live on the street.

Kenneth Till

LICHFIELD

You approved of Lichfield. It was 'self-contained'
You said. A guided tour of fog-swathed streets,
Cramped cafes, and bleak winter ducks cold-shouldering
The ice brought only smiles from you. The spires
Protruding from the mist's embrace were all you saw
Of the cathedral, yet its beauty still impressed.
The stamp of your goodwill has hallmarked this city,
My home, ever since. You franked it with your pleasure.

And when you died, one hundred miles away up the M6,
Your feisty spirit tailed me home and lodged here,
Nesting unbidden in the memory's lofty branches.
Lichfield. Literally *'field of the dead'*. I imagine
Your wraith, constant and benign, one of thousands
Thronging the triple spires with particular blessings.

Jane Redman

IN OUR HOUSE

We have creatures with no faces
That move around
And don't leave traces,
As they flit from room to room
Why do I have
A sensation of doom,
Why are they here?
Their very presence
Fills me with fear.
Now they are gathering
And surround me
What are they doing
What can it be?
Then I realise it is the time
Of my rebirth,
The last day in this life
I shall spend in earth.

The Fossil

WHAT A MESS

The chimneys are blowing out, horrible smoke,
From the burning of nuclear waste,
the air is full of pesticides,
being sprayed all over the place.
There's foul smelling rivers, all killing the fish,
pollution is rife, so it seems,
and I don't think it's what was intended,
not in my wildest dreams.
Traffic congestion, is filling the roads
with fumes, we all breathe, every day.
Motorways getting longer,
poisonous air getting stronger,
I don't fancy the price, we shall pay.
There's funny things, floating round space,
There's a hole, in the Ozone layer,
Goodness knows, what will happen next,
We should all be saying a prayer. . .
Everyone's pushing and shoving,
No time, it seems to stand still,
There's even some folk, that I know of,
Say they haven't got time to be ill.
Well I can't help but wonder sometimes
if the old days, were not the best,
When we weren't all blinded, by science,
And everyone, knew how to rest.
It's all in the name of progress,
but it don't seem that way to me
The poor old world's being ruined
in the name of technology.

But folks had better watch out. . .
One day we'll be put to the test
For we are just tenants in this world.
And the 'Land Lord' knows what's best.

Jacqueline Claire Davies

THE GREAT DIVIDE

This day to Biddulph moor we went,
To where a meagre trickle spawned.
The meandering River Trent,
Through midland towns it mourned.

This is the source from which,
Amongst the watercress,
And emergence without a hitch,
To begin its hallowed wish.

To sweep across the breadth of England,
The great divide of north and south,
As though Merlin waves his wand,
And set course for the river mouth.

Bestowing its name on a city,
A few short miles from its head,
To be polluted by an industrial society
As the mills and factories spread.

The agrarian scenario gives way,
To a belching pot bellied oven,
And the midlands accents belay,
To all that need it proven.

The long Trent valley we deduct,
The haunt of many a northern bird,
Curlew, Merlin and the tufted duck,
Along the banks, is often heard.

Now the source of pollution is reducing,
The river flows with a new vitality,
The process of rehabilitation is swelling,
And is refurbished to its originality.

Raymond Baggaley

PEER GROUP PARADE

The rhythm of the band
Depends on the co-operation of my peers
And those with the loudest voice
Influence every members tune

The base drum who knows it all
Tough and inflexible with a booming voice
Less courageous members beat to his tune
Drowning those instruments whose notes waver

The woodwind section plods on reliably
Clarinets and flutes who continue at their own pace
Oblivious to trends, unswayed by opinions
Trumpets and cornets who stamp out their own tune
Confident enough to take the lead if only given a chance

Then there are the waverers
Triangles and symbols, sleigh bells and maracas
Holding fire to determine the lie of the land
Then rushing in at the last minute to secure the safest bet

The peer group parade
To spectators full of wonderful entertainment
Whilst its members struggle to find their pace
Within the harmony of every song

Jill Ison

MY DAD

My dad is just the bravest,
The bravest as can be,
He really is a tough guy,
But wouldn't hurt a flea.

When I was going to take a bath,
A spider made me shout,
My dad came to keep me company,
While mum threw it out.

When we heard noises downstairs,
When it was very late,
Dad came to hide in my room,
While mum went to investigate.

I knew you'd need protecting,
He whispered in my ear,
He's all and more than I'll ever need,
A superdad with no fear.

Laura Smith

DRIFTING

Words, however innocent they
Sound,
Like drifting snowflakes
Build a mound
That outwardly seems
Pure and right,
Yet those same words
Are shafts of light
Whose heat, exposing,
Melts the mound,
Revealing there,
Upon the ground
Old scars.

David Edwards

MORE THAN SKIN DEEP

People take you at face value
And never look for the underneath
They never know
Who you really are

Underneath, you are a completely
Different person, an individual.
Underneath the exterior is
Another person trying to get out

Under the skin, is your
Sensitive side, the side you only
Show to your closest,
Nearest and dearest

If people were to look deeper,
To go further than face value
They would find that you
Are a totally different person.

Daniel Parton

CHILDREN

These days children do not dare
To wander far from mother's care
Dangers lurk upon our roads
Lorries with their heavy loads.

High powered cars go speeding past
Motor cycles just as fast
Joy riders fleeing from police
Is there never any peace?

Parks and playgrounds can hold danger
One day there may be a stranger
Who would lure a child from play
To go with him far away.

Bullies always are around
In the childrens' own school ground
Where can children safely play?
It seems there is nowhere today.

Edna Perry

MY DEAR FRIEND

Dear Lord, please bless my friend, she is in so much despair
Let her know I'm there for her, and let her know I care
Show me how to comfort her, and to show to her your peace
Let her know Your love and care, from her, you'll never leave

Let me show compassion, and this burden help her bear
This grief that she carries, I want with her to share
Please help me show my love for her, and to show I understand
When she needs somebody, I'll be there to hold her hand

I want so much to give her peace, and show my friendship true
I want her to know she's not alone, as this heart ache she goes through
Lord take this grief away from her, free her from her pain
Let her know you always will, by her side remain

You are the Comforter, Our Shepherd up above
I know in you, she will have peace, by resting in Your love
So may she feel You ever near, Your peace to her now give
That you are with her always, ever more, that she may live

Jean Beardshore

LONELINESS

A little old lady sits by the fire,
The flame is so tiny it's about to expire
No-one to come in or a kiss or a cuddle
No-one to care that the room's in a muddle
An old man sits on a bench by the lake
The wind blows cold, and his old bones ache.
No-one awaits in his one dreary room
With a hug and a smile to chase off the gloom.
Somewhere a boy asks him mum, 'Where's my nan?'

And a girl asks her dad, 'Is your dad an old man?'
Consciences prick and door bells ring
Loneliness is forgotten, old hearts start to sing.
When they were your age those years long ago
They were the ones who welcomed you home
To a lovely bright room, and a nice cup of tea
So a smile, and a chat, and the odd job or two
Are a small price to pay
To stop old folk feeling blue.

N Gosling

SHELLS ON THE HILLS

Breathless from the climb,
I stop at an explosion
of stones tracing the
pattern of a farmhouse.

A skim of moss and lichen
creep over the scattered
remains absorbing it slowly
to a shallow unmarked grave.

Clusters of stones begging
an answer and snarling
their silent rage.

Eira Williams

THOUGHTS AT CHRISTMAS

It's Christmas time again,
remember those in pain,
the ones without the means,
to realise their dreams.
The ones who are underprivileged
aged or infirm,
think of those without the cash to burn.
Remember in your thoughts
those stripped of all they own,
victims of war and violence,
not too far away from home.
There's drought and flood and pestilence
both here and overseas,
men, women and children riddled with disease.
Let's offer help where help is needed,
don't allow their cries to go unheeded.
We're all involved, yes, you and me!
Remove your blinkers then you'll see,
sit up, react, make a donation,
this is not the time for procrastination,
Christmas is a celebration,
forget the religious connotation.
The Human nation, yes, all of us
must work together, make a fuss
and help those less well off,
it may be us not them, be warned,
the day to realise has dawned.

Gary Westwood

WHEN ONE BECOMES TWO

Oh! Those early years
When we thought of ourselves as one
Then came that fateful day
When the illusion was gone.

Born to have shared name
To grow up together
One of us is now old
The other perhaps never.

The old one is often tired
Suffers aches and pain
Legs and joints stiffened
Never to skip to school again.

We are inseparable
But what an odd pair we now make
One would go on and on
The other ever slowing, slowing, applying the brake.

When we watch Wimbledon tennis
One has us chasing every ball
With effortless ease
We are there in no time at all.

When match is over
There is a painful journey to make
From armchair to 'telly'
Another yard slower if there's added backache.

Age brings experience
There is much we might do
If vitality was for life
Not for those early years few.

C E Hooper

THE SEAGULL

I have held a seagull in my hands
It wasn't Jonathan Livingstone
How could it be
But
I held something wild and free
Impossible to imagine
And
Just for that moment
Small heartbeat
Lost and turning to me
Everything else forgotten
No time
Just now

This life
Follows where the heart must go
I have held a seagull in my arms
As the buses roared by
And the cars thundered past
Just for that moment
Time stood still
And we two
Lost wild and free
Everything else forgotten
Looked to one another
And believed
That we would somehow survive
All this
And fly away forever

Della Roberts

DESTRUCTION

It's hard to watch old age at work
Destroying what you've known.
It's sad to see eyes blank or dead,
A person all alone,
Somehow cut off from daily life,
A mind no longer working,
A world cut down to just four walls.
A brain with strange thoughts lurking.
How can we understand the change?
Much harder, how accept it?
The loved one changed, the feelings drained,
- So hard not to condemn it.
You're torn apart by little things -
They don't know who you are,
They think they've just been down the street
Or riding in a car,
When really, they've been nowhere
And there's nowhere else to go.
What a tragic end to life.
How they feel, we'll never know.

M A Butcher

CHRISTMAS NIGHT

Christmas bells are ringing out on the still clear night,
Pealing out a song of joy, a Saviour born tonight,
Crisp and deep the snow is laying,
Stars glitter in the sky.
All the heavens with joy are ringing,
The Christ child born tonight.

May the joy that Christmas brings,
Linger in our hearts,
Bringing peace and joy to all men,
On this hallowed night.

Thank you Lord for blessing given,
The blessing of your Son,
May the joy that Christmas brings,
In our hearts abide.

Rose Horleston

THE LECTURE

In ventricular motion, the doors are opened
A flow of fresh faces each take their place
The gentle boil of conversation, growing,
While others keep the beat sustained
As if injected, a man struggles in
Face sullen and distorted
'Let the lesson begin'

Of all of us present, few understood
The clotting rhetoric, though respect could see
The lines on his face, engrained in the wood
Rooted firmly in Eden, his body a tree
'I bear this fruit, take it for thee'

Soon all was over
Once more the flow restored
Ahead, the world, anaemically sleeping
Fruit in our minds, and seeds in our hands.

Simon Pennicott

UNIQUE

What do I see from the window,
The place I've known so long.
The same trees will always grow,
And the people I've lived among.
But I'm not like the others,
Why do they all act the same?
Influenced by sisters and brothers,
I prefer the person I became.
I'm not the same as the rest,
Forever I want to be me.
Being myself is always best,
My spirit will always be free.

Louise Spears

SHAUN

To Shaun I'd say put it away,
Sit down, be quiet, you hear what I say.
You're only five, not eighteen,
You talk to much, it's all a dream.
How could I have such a clever boy,
How come you've brought us so much joy.
Sometimes you're a bit too clever
For this lady to endeavour.
You're two steps ahead of me all the time,
Hyperactive, it's not a crime.
Just carry on, pull it out,
I'll have to bite my lip not to shout.
Stand up and talk all you like,
When you leave home, it'll be too quiet.

K Biggs

STILLNESS

In the stillness of the forest
I sit down by the stream
Watching the flowing waters
As I begin to dream

And as I look around me
Tall pines reach to the sky
The fragrance from the meadow
And a lark singing on high

Birds are busy nesting
In those tall pines up above
As I dream of you my darling
Just to hold you and to love

As I gaze into the water
Just gently flowing by
Dreaming of the memories
My love of you and I

My love for you is flowing
Just like the waters there
The sunrays beams shine from above
As I just dream and stare

The stillness and the beauty
I long to share with you
The day we take our vows my love
The day you say I do

G Thomas

A MOTHER'S LOVE

The seed is planted at conception
gradually over nine months it grows
until that momentous hour when
the fruit of your love to the world its face shows.

All at once you are smitten
by the greatest love of your life
now nature has made you a mother
no longer just somebody's wife.

You feel a sense of wonder
at the miracle of nature through mother earth
relief is overwhelming
for this child so perfect to which you've given birth.

when your child suckles the bonding is complete
feelings so strong you feel quite weak
but this magnitude of love
you'll never feel again wherever you seek.

Suddenly it hits you like a bolt between the eyes
no matter what the future holds or the life they lead
you'll love protect and care for them
give them everything they need.

They are every beat of your heart
they live within each intake of breath
and only one thing will ever separate you
the inevitability of death.

Susan Hunter

MY ISLAND

Back in Mayo on the West Coast
That paradise place by the sea
When I visit its tang comes to meet me
It's my homeland saying *failte* to me.

Nothing changes in that beautiful island
Its peatbogs, its mountains nor sea
It exudes a mysterious magic
And will always be heaven to me.

In the rugged landscape and fields of wild heather
Where time itself seems to stand still
There are curlews and corncrakes still nesting
In meadows of cowslip, buttercup and cranesbill.

Pontoon with its woods and its valleys
Its rocky plains, boglands and streams
Beautifully evoking a lost peace and tranquillity
With its scenic and geological extremes.

Hunting clouds and soft mists all there mingle
With surf-fringed beaches and blue hurtling streams
Amidst heather bells, fern and green bushes
In this enchanting old island of dreams.

Some day I'll return to this haven
My Eden perched right by the sea
To my soft green hills and high mountains
Or could this be just the dreamer in me?

Mary C Soden

MOM - DAD

Dangling in the wind
      dripping in the rain
You can't explain your feelings
      So start pleading insane.

You can't explain your reasons
      and tell them what to do
because they will say they're older
      and it's only what you would do

The place you once knew as home
      and where you grew up,
know only a distance memorise a dream
      from which you've woken up

Doing your best and doing what
      they say, you know what you
want them to do, but it's impossible
      for them to stay.

That once close-knit feeling
      Has now pulled apart
What once made me happy
      Has now broke my heart

So sickly feeling from deep down inside
      stop showing your hurt
because there's no broken pride.

N G Shaw

THE VISIT
(Written in the 'voice' of a Downs Syndrome Child)

I did not ask to come
Nor warn you of my coming
But I am here.

I too brought gifts
The gold of my unselfish love
The frankincense of my serenity
And myrrh for comforting your grief.

My needs are small
My place lies hidden from the eye
That cannot see
My place in our eternity.

I see the clouds
I sense the storms
I too know pain
But I am blessed with joy
And that is why I came.

Marie Cope

ROBERT

I held you in my arms that morn,
When away from me you had been torn.
Your tiny hands, your tiny feet,
The little heart that ceased to beat.
I held you close to say goodbye,
The pain inside, I could not cry.
I laid you down upon your bed,
Tenderly caressed your little head.
Your face, your hair were all the same,
I wished inside you'd breathe again.
They came with haste and took you away,
A piece of me left with you that day.
I could not accept what God had done,
I love you Robert my only son.

Suzanne Hoare

TO JOYCE

I just don't want the evening to end,
Sitting here with you my friend,
Quiet, in the companionship,
Linked in love and related,
By the joint cup we sip.

Together by the sighing of the fire,
Supporting things we both did sire,
Things of lifes' times, tears and dedication,
We relax, both of us in reparation,
Within the comfort of our relation.

The warming sound of passing train,
Gets joined in fun by the tapping rain,
Mad wind outside squalls, 'A train, - chase!'
You quietly placing washing by the fireplace,
So comforting with your smiling face.

All of these things assure me of,
An ever, ever lasting love.

Stephen Poller

ON THE SLEEPING CHILDREN IN LICHFIELD CATHEDRAL

How delicate they look in sleep,
Fashioned in marble by an early hand,
These two sweet innocents, their arms entwined
In love and pure content.
Snatched from a life of love and joy,
- and in her hand one with a posy bent -
One of a fever died, and one by fire.

And so their Mother, wrought with grief,
despatched with haste a local man
A sculptor, to Ashbourne Church to see
An effigy of one - a younger child,
Deep in sleep on cushioned comfort laid.
She wished her daughters too, might thus be formed,
To live forever in remembrance.

Centuries must pass and still their youth and freshness will remain,
Reminding those who gaze, love never dies,
So, through two 'C's', a sculptor's art, and writer's hand,
They live for all, into eternity.

Jean Quance

PLATES

We eat off them
We break them
And from where I come from
We even make them

We collect them
We treasure them
And do our best
To protect them

We use them to commemorate
We use them to celebrate
So we should never underate
The uses of the humble plate

We display and array them
We find them even in the hallway
Infact in anyway, I wonder
What we would do without the plate.

Margaret A Stonier

PROSTHETICS

By the time you hear there'll only be a glimmer
of the truth remaining.
      We all know the ending of the
story of the bloke out gardening
who sheared off his foot with a strimmer.
With no-one in earshot, no-one at home,
he had to hop to the nearest pay-phone
and an operator who'd heard it all
(she thought, until she took this call
and the particulars). She had to gag
at the leg-stump swabbed with an oily rag
and the foot God knows where.
The ambulance found him at the pub on the corner,
nursing a bucket; an ice-cube container
that got carried away at arm's length.

It's all bollocks of course. I've a strimmer of my own
and could show you how the plastic whirr
might cut an ankle to the bone
but no way any further.
And anyway, you see the shaft is
twice as long as your average leg is -
it's like hitting the hand holding the truncheon -
impossibly designed for self-mutilation.
And you'd be a chip short of a butty
to keep your throttle finger clenched
having had your flesh lashed.
Of course, there is a catch. . .
      The foot?
It arrived in the bucket toes still twitching
and after five hours of surgical stitching
it came out whole with catgut embroidery.

He played football that Sunday.

David Ellerton (Deceased)

THE BOOK

It all started with a bit of luck,
When Robert Fleck published his book.
The book it was a real scare,
You it would fright I honestly swear.

He had written the book awfully well,
So as a result it began to sell.
Millions of people brought the story.
Even though it was a little gory.

A top producer thought the book was groovy,
He wanted to make it into a movie.
Robert, oh how he jumped at the chance,
He was over the moon and began to dance.

The film was released and was a big hit,
So the money kept on coming in bit by bit.
It appeared to be going very well,
But he was just about to enter hell.

For the book was taking over people's minds,
And making them do evil things of all kinds.
They seemed to be on a different level,
As if they were possessed by the devil.

The days passed by without any glory,
As the papers got hold of his story.
It all got too much he just couldn't cope,
So he killed himself with the aid of a rope.

The funeral went ahead in days
And people just carried on with their ways.
No-one cared that he was not around,
After all he was 6ft under the ground.

His wife didn't even cry or bellow,
For she had got another fellow.

Mark Hipwell (13)

REALITY AND SYMPATHY

When you met me, what did you see
The person, the man, or the HIV?
Did you ponder on where I got it from
And how many months before I'd be gone.
Is my lover to blame, or a suspect transfusion
Or the needle that washed me in waves of confusion?
In spite of all your urge to see
You'll never know what infected me.
I won't give you the pleasure, gossip monger
To share concerned looks over cups of tea
And make arrangements for a burial at sea.
You see once, long ago, I had a life
A car, 2.4, a house and a wife
I know you'll find it hard to accept my fate
But I'm still alive and it's not too late.
Don't patronise or pity me.
The saviour is reality.
Look at me and then you'll see
A fact of life infected me.
The reality
A fact of our lives infected me.

Julian Devereux

URBAN FOX

Midnight and moonlight
Foxes are about
Searching the dustbins
For fast food, no doubt.

Several times just lately
My bin has been upturned
The garden strewn with litter
A cause for great concern,

But hopefully this nuisance
Will soon be at an end
When wheelie bins are issued
What will urban fox do then?

Bet he will think of something
Devious I'll be bound
And wheelie bin with lid half cocked
Will be tumbled to the ground.

Amelia Canning

HIROSHIMA

Shocked, scared. These innocents'
Glazed eyes stare, and memories
Repeat themselves over and over.
Before the light was seen they were fine.
Now the nightmare is trapped
Inside heads of melted skin,
And the sea of pain ebbs its way
To a shore of sorrow and loss.
Men writhe in agony
As their hollowed eyes try to weep
And their wounded lips utter no sound.
A child feeds from its mother's breast,
His tiny body scarred and blistered.
No-one is too young. No-one is too old,
And the pain is infinite.
Even the inao has been chased by scorching flames.
Behind the wall of suffering
A tumult of questions and numb emotions mix
To form gnawing grief. As the city fell,
So did the hearts of the people.

Kate Herd

NOVEMBER INCIDENT

Today was the selling of poppies
Not the naming of parts.
Just the selling of poppies

I saw the seller by the door
Cold and pink-tipped.
With tin and muffler, smiling at me.

No change - I fumble - but of course
A coin trapped in the lining
I find with relief.

Does it matter or count
Do the young know
The meaning in the black and red.

The toddler pleased and important
Is pinning it into his coat
Turning at the rattling of the tin.

O God, I think as I sweep
Through the doors of the supermarket,
What did they die for?

What does it really mean now?
Just the cenotaph, the flags, the Albert Hall
And of course, the falling of poppies.

J Curlett

THE AGONIES OF DECEPTION

Lying here, I pick up the album,
And my eye stops on one photo -
You, dressed in white, smiling,
Radiant in the late summer sunshine -
A moment caught in time.

Now, split asunder,
Tears prick at your eyes
As you recall the happy event
And all that led to it.
Now your mind is flooded with memories,
What the guests wore or did,
Remembering what your mother said,
And in the end how right she was.

Did it really take so long
To realise the mortar
That held you together
Was merely sand,
Which now has finally washed away.

Chris Davies

A SHORT EXTRACT OF LIFE

Life is what you make it
Build it, and treasure it
You can't guarantee it
So make the most of it
It is very easy to say life is
Shit or in the pits
But it is not easy to try and
Realise why it is like this.
Even so, life is given to us
And sadly taken away from
Us for mysterious destinations
We should share it with
Every friend to conclude
A happy end.

Kulbir Sharni

SNOOTY SWANS

On the river swans afloat
Dignified, remote
From common mallard, teal and scoter
They could not be remoter.
One says: 'My neck is like a slender stem
I can't associate with them.'
And, looking down his snooty beak,
'With likes of that lot, I won't speak.
Those ducks lack elegance and poise
Their quacking makes a dreadful noise.
As to those hoards of Canada geese
Will their honking never cease?
Just what are things coming to?
It's worse than living in a zoo.
Come, pen, we'll quietly glide down stream
And find a place serene and clean
And there in rushes, out of sight,
We'll rear our cygnets to be polite.'

Joan Ierston

LINEN

Fabricated skin
Nothing to be gained by me
Always something in it for you
Creased in
Ironed thin
The stain holds fast on my threaded
sustain

Calico
Impure, yet clean
Rid of this static state
A stark reminder of almost certainty

Length ways we hold no width
A depth without character
Disturb the stitch, the blood runs
clean
Needle and thread contain the thoughts
Linen contains the thinking

Paul Coles

SMALL WONDER

From the very first day when the doctor says yes,
and you bid fond farewell to your favourite dress.
You wonder.

Aunties, sisters and cousins with patterns galore,
supply hats, coats and bootees to fill every drawer.
Though you say 'That's enough,' they keep sending you more,
and He wonders.

With the nursery 'done out' in a pale, neutral hue,
and you hope you've done everything there is to do.
You sit quietly down and together review
if everything said about parenthood's true.
And you both wonder.

Then the great day arrives and they whisk you away
to a different world filled with whiteness and grey.
From the depths of despair, to a pinnacle high,
every sense re-awakens to a shrill, piercing cry
as they hand you the product of nine months gone by.
And the world . . . *Wonders.*

Elizabeth E Smullen

TWILIGHT

I've flown through the sky
I've sailed across the sea
I've gazed at distant stars
In all their glory.

I've climbed the high mountains
Spent much time alone
Reached out for far distant dreams
But I've never felt 'home.'

So now here I am
Alone I am still
I must go on searching
Search then I will.

I may never find
The peace that I seek
But I must keep on going
Though hope now grows weak.

And then when finally
In the end I'm no more
I hope I have given back
To those I lived for
A little of the caring
That they gave to me
That they may know
I will love them forever
Through all eternity.

Tony Smith

THE WORLD AS ONE

If the world, loved as one,
We could really have some fun.
No arguments about creed or race,
No fights over, your colour of face.
The money that once paid for war,
Could buy some food, to feed the poor.
No scraps at the football, wouldn't that be great.
Two opposing fans, could call each other mate.
There'd be no hassle, between man and wife,
They could live together and enjoy their life.
We would only use drugs to cure disease,
And we would recycle paper to save our trees.
We'd put an end to the rainforests being cut down,
And we'd stop pollution in our town.
We'd save the whale, the kangaroo,
White rhino, bald eagle and the elephant too.
No rich countries playing the power game,
And no third world, 'cos we'd all be the same.
Whether black, white or yellow,
We would call each other brother,
We could live in harmony,
And laugh and joke with one another,
About the bad old days,
When all we did was fight,
And how living in peace,
Every thing seems right.
But alas it's a dream, if only it was true,
The world would be a better place to live,
For the likes of me and you.

Dave 'Snapper' Snape

CERTIFIED INSANE

Madness

They stop and stare
Mock and jeer
Abnormality, imperfection
Subnormal, inhuman
Judge him wrapped
In poisoned prejudice
Lock and imprison
Scorn, spit, chase
Ice it in social etiquette
To be accepted
In the charade
We term society.

Say he has no emotion,
Say he is incapable,
To love or hate
To be loved,
To belong.

Strangle his existence
Say he is not worthy
To share your world
Do you understand
The darkened prison?
For you exiled him there
Yes, you and your world
Or self righteousness
And walled 'normality'
Are you normal?
Or are you to be

Certified Insane?

Rita Pal

DEATH OF A FAMILY DOG

It is a sad occasion when your hearts break in two,
The dog who has grown up with your children
Is no longer there with you.
Mourning can be such a hard time -
Some people simply cannot see
That the death of an old canine friend
Hurts like death in humanity.

No water bowl needs refilling,
Throw the tins of dog food all away,
Forget about the biscuits that she loved,
She died the day before yesterday,
The lead that hangs in the kitchen
Will not be needed anymore,
Her collar and disc are hidden out of sight
Somewhere in the kitchen drawer.

'It is for the best,' people tell you,
And although it may ring true
It does not help the pain of loss
Because she belonged to you.

Weeks pass by, hurt still remains,
You see her though she is no longer there,
You find you cannot speak her name
And you feel nothing is ever fair.
You are kind and give a home
To a needy dog who may come your way the same,
And years on you will be sobbing
And going through it all again.

M C Eggleton

AN ALBUM FOR CHRISTMAS

Picture this:

A war torn city besieged by fear,
Daily facing death and destruction,
A desolate existence of danger and despair
Where raging thunderstorms
And lighting flashes
Rain down bombs and bullets
Upon innocent victims,
All in the name of religion.

Picture this:

A moving mass of human debris,
The shipwrecked remains of persecuted people
Seeking shelter from starvation and suffering,
Their emaciated, deformed bodies
Too weak to cry for help
Or curse this deprivation and disease forced
Upon innocent victims,
All in the name of politics.

Picture this:

A portrait of poverty and degradation,
The social outcasts of the cardboard culture;
Citizens stripped of their dignity,
Forced to live like animals.
Foraging and begging for food
Whilst affluence and greed prosper, growing fat
Upon innocent victims,
All in the name of profit.

Picture this and remember:

Peace and goodwill to all men
All in the name of humanity.

Mary Hyland

DOOR TO DOOR SALESMEN

Take a minute to read before you ring my bell,
I'm not interested in what you have to sell.
I wouldn't just sit about and wait,
For you to come through my front gate.
I'd let my fingers do the walking,
Pick up the phone and do some talking.
Now think twice before you try to flog,
I'll warn you that I've got a dog.

E Taylor

SEXTH COLUMN

When there's a dearth of floods and wrecks,
We turn to that old standby, 'Sex'
Always guaranteed in favour,
If presented with a raunchy flavour.
Although it's practised every night,
(ten billion couples must be right,)
In every attitude and way,
From Budapest to old Bombay,
And from the privacy of home,
To cat houses in arctic Home,
And down the years to ancient Greece,
On or under the Golden Fleece,
Yet the weeklies and the dailies claim
That what they offer is not the same.
The only difference, I proclaim,
Is in *whom* you choose to share the game.

Alan N Marshall

MY BEST FRIEND

The tears of joy rest upon you,
The shadows of love within you.
You help me in a way unreal,
To help me cope, you help me feel -
The life you share to keep me be,
Can only through my eyes see.
The true beauty of life within this world,
On the grasp of dreams you can but unhold.
The secret of hopes you feel here,
Can only reveal in desperate fear.
To share, to hold, to be, to see,
Is the greatest thing you can find in me.

Ann Marie Hinds

MATERNAL GRATITUDE

The slender bond that held us once,
Is strengthened now beyond your control,
I was yours to nurture, in times now gone,
Yet forever I will still need you.

My past memories belong only to you,
Of warm laughter, life protected and sated,
No dark memories can ever live,
Whilst you stand guard within my life.

Other people stand near now,
But none has a life so clear,
Blurred people smiling, sharing amusement,
Your smile still clear and loving.

The years have moved onward now,
In some eyes I have moved toward manhood,
Within yours I am still a helpless child.
Bewildered and blissfully dependent.

My life now created from you,
Guidance forming deep morality,
Advice will survive through ages to come,
From you to me to my own.

Steven McLuckie

WRITER'S BLOCK

I have a case of writer's block,
I think I'll go and eat some choc (olate).
I'm sitting here, I'd rather not
Outside the weather's nice and hot.
'Write a poem quick!' my mind hissed -
I'd rather write a shopping list!
A jar of jam
An ounce of ham
A packet of jelly
Deodorant (smelly)
Vegetable soup
Spaghetti hoops
And of course
Mustard (coarse).
I'm sorry if I bored you but,
At least I'm not stuck in a rut!

Alison Walters

GRAINS

There is complexity even in simplicity,
this is the art of design.

Sweep a jack-plane over wood
and there is design.

Beech grain is heavy rain
blurring Gothic castles in misty cloud.

Cherrywood, light and bright,
is rock crystal with succulent fruit.

Elm is a ripe harvest field of corn stalks,
tinted a copra plantation in the sun.

Oak is varnish in thick variation
like treacle oozing along a wet table.

Pine has a huge single eye
like Cyclops watching an incoming tide.

Rosewood is patterned obscurely,
like a sombre robed judge in corridors.

Sapele is milk and plain chocolate on trays,
like cirrocumulus sky at late sunset.

Walnut is darkful, glossy patches
mirroring coffee cups like cloudy glass.

Zebrawood - as you readily guess - is
zig-zag stripy, deep brown sandstone: a donkey!

Dennis Marshall

REDISCOVERING LOLLIPOP STICKS

And summer rolled out its carpet
On the swoop of the green hill.
We charged into battle.
Through broad whistles of grass
And the fox dented straw
We rolled and laughed over
                      and over
                                  and over
Stopping.

On the stile
Where he had seen the Northern Lights,
We stepped dusty footed
Into his dog days.

Red birthday sandals with semolina soles
Slap their happy slap
Between high hedgerows mumbling of autumn
Where cow parsley rocks in the breeze
Shaking a snow heavy head in sorrow
For moments that cannot last.

On now to Dirty Foot lane.
We hide our lollipop sticks in hedges,
Like gypsies,
Swearing oaths to retread paths,
Research, refind,
These relics of a special time.

Now vague

Emma Purshouse

THE SMILE

She didn't try to stop him killing her
She was an artist after all
So she took it in the back
Blade between the blades
Like a true professional
Eyes averted, lips parted
Fixing her last expression
To intrigue infinitely

She didn't try to stop him killing her
She was an artist after all
So she took it in the back
Blade between the blades
Like a true professional
Saving herself the job
Twenty years later
She only hoped he remembered
To kill himself
Like all decent passion killers
After
She didn't want any loose ends
Spoiling the pathos
Any question of her bewitchment
Any risk of her obscurity
Among domestics

She didn't try to stop him killing her
She was an artist after all
And she made great art.

L S King

THE CHANGING SEASONS

Spring is like a baby's birth
When buds of life emerge
The earth awakens from its sleep
And rivers cease to surge

The spun-gold sun comes out to play
And flowers begin to bloom
Blue skies instead of grey appear
To lighten winter's gloom

The summer's likened to the young
Maturing as they grow
With sunbeam dancing round their feet
Their faces all aglow

Sweet balmy nights to fall in love
Stars dazzling in their eyes
Warm sand against the ebbing tide
And breeze that gently sighs

Autumn comes with leaves of gold
And gently sheds its tears
The sun sets in blue velvet skies
Just like maturing years

The winter months are long and hard
Yet spring is ever nigh
Old age can rest from life's cruel scene
And watch the snowflakes fly

The changing seasons of our lives
Are filled with smiles and tears
But we should savour every hour
'Cause hours soon turn to years.

Jackie Thornton

PERFUNCTORY FACTORIES MECHANICAL MEN

Resolute numb, un-complaining men,
Look at their calloused hands.
Primitive workers, grimed up to their eyes,
In production line factories stand.
Closed are the pits, closed the mines,
Gone, the pipe-works, and steel.
Look at their faces, of furrowed toil,
See in their eyes, how they feel.
Strong men who labour, doing what bids,
With backbone, they do not shirk,
Some looked broken bent and scarred,
Everything hard, but headwork.
Perfunctory factories, mechanical men,
Creating masters rich,
Standing in line, working in time,
Producing to the end of the shift.
Friday's the day, when masters pay,
Last week of daily hire,
Work for the workers, statesmen say,
Will return us, from the mire.
Biddings been done, pocketing their sum,
See how in line they stand,
Perfunctory factories, mechanical men,
Judged, by the work of their hands.

David Vanter

LAMENT OF THE UNIVERSE

I am older than time,
yet as fresh as the dawn.
The sum of a rainbow
after a storm.

I'm as young as the babe
breaking through the womb's door.
In Me is found wisdom,
laughter and tears.

I support all the planets,
protect life from the Jaws
of the Cast Iron Dogs
who live to make wars.

Dorothy Bell-Hall

THE WORD

In the beginning was the word,
And the Lord moved over the face of the word,
And the word went singing through the blades of grass,
Hiding logic from the eyes of men.

At the ceremonies of men
The word howled,
Stamped on the earth,
Looked stubborn.

Then, in the company of wolves,
The word became silent,
And hid
In a barrel of smoke.

The word became cunning,
And sang to itself a little
Of lost songs, and lost wars.

In the beginning was the word,
And the Lord moved over the face of the word,
And the word went singing through the blades of grass.

Paul Williams

DEAFNESS

. . . I'm cut off from conversation!
I try so hard to hear your words,
Yet I miss words, which means that the conversation
doesn't make sense.
I am easily made aware that something's not right,
because of the puzzled look on the face of the other person.
Do they think that I'm not too intelligent?
If only they could experience what I'm feeling . . .
If only for a day!
I may appear to be an embarrassment to others when
they are forced to talk in a loud voice in company.
In fact, it's better to speak softly . . . it produces better results!
I can see the irritation on the faces when I haven't understood . . .
and it hurts! . . . I'm not to blame for my disability!
I would gladly change places with you at any time.
Please remember I'm a person first and deaf last!
I'm still aware of things around me . . .
Please don't presume that I've lost my intellect because I'm deaf.
I still have my skills despite deafness, but I show them in a different way.
If you want to communicate with me, please face me and talk slowly, in
order that both parties may be understood.
If this practice is adhered to . . . what pleasure it creates!

Sandra Bache

ROLL . . . UP . . . THE . . . FLAG

Roll up the flag to the roll of the drum,
The banner is raised the task must be won;
There are many things for a dreadful purge,
In everyone's heart a compelling urge.

'Tis God who makes peace, 'Tis God who makes war,
For 'tis God's own reason not human law;
The people on earth their banners are hailed,
Yet the people on earth have always failed.

The evil of humans just as they come,
All people are sinners under the sun;
All the war leaders with all of their might,
But it's only God who can put things right.

The pleasant land made to a battle field
With all the terror that a war can wield;
Roll up the flag to the roll of the drum,
The banner is raised the task must be won.

Dennis Parkes Rowley Regis

MY GARDEN OF FRIENDSHIP

When I walk in my garden I think of you
And like the plants our friendship grew,
For I have a garden of friendship you see
I name plants after friends who give them to me.

Beneath the honeysuckle almost in shade
Grow miniature roses called Masquerade,
These were a gift from a friend so dear
I feel so sad she is not here.

For she was called to God's garden above
To tend heavenly flowers with her love,
In my garden of friendship where I love to roam
Grow miniature roses, I call them Joan.

When I walk in my garden I think of you
And like the plants our friendship grew,
I have a garden of friendship you see
Where each plant holds a sweet memory.

Mary Amelia Payne

THE FIVE SENSES

Seeing
What graceful beauty in a tree,
A dream of bloss'ming ecstacy,
Whose willowy fronds of emerald lace
Down-kiss the placid water's face,
O'er all fair things on earth - a tree
is quite the loveliest to see.

Hearing:
What joy in the song of a bird,
A matin without e'er a word,
Harmonic trills of flute-like grace
Catch up the breath, pause, go on apace.
I've heard sweet prima-donnas sing,
Better - the lark's song on the wing.

Smelling:
The wallflower perfume's heaven blent,
Waft me the Queen-of-Velvet scent,
I love the fragrant rose and musk,
Sweet honeysuckle in the dusk,
Lilac, lime-trees, or clover plot,
But breathe a wallflower-scented grot.

Tasting:
Nature evolved the good for man,
In divers tastes, Creation's plan,
Sweet or bitter a taste whereby
Acception or rejection lie,
Man selects his food by flavour,
Eating fruits he loves to savour.

Touching:
The caress of a loving hand,
Transports us to another land,
Where kindred hearts and souls do dwell
And without words have much to tell,
Such feeling howsoever light
Expresses love in all its might.

Theo James

MY CITY

They say it's the second city, I think it's second to none,
You'll find it in the Midlands, close to England's heart, that's Brum,
No, It's not in Alabama, or places round the globe
We call it Birmingham City, my city, in Europe we're well know,
We boast plenty of performers, politicians famous names,
Opera's are the norm, in a place they call the convention centre,
And the acoustics' there can cause a storm,
We have a mermaid in the fountain, she can be found in the old square,
Better take your dark-glasses for she's big and she's bare,
Down in the Bull-Ring markets, the traders they are great,
You can buy diamond rings, to anything and veg'ies by the crate,
We've got Aston Villa Football club, I'm sure they are well know,
And The Blues, Birmingham City's own.
Now down the road, a yard or two, if you think you've lost your head,
It's lying in the heartland's its nose painted blue, its ear to the ground,
They say it's listening to the city's heart, every pulsating sound,
Just out of town, there's the NEC it is the place o be, for Crufts,
Fashion and stuff, the motor-show is the thing you'll want to see,
After the art museums, are multi-culture, by our citizens of multi-race,
Nip across to St Philips churchyard, there's lots of benches to ease a
                                                                     back-ache.
We'll say, 'Yo'mm an't aw'f a good bloke.' and that's no joke.
Come on pay us a visit, in Birmingham City there's no limit.

Joan McAvoy

A WARTIME CHRISTMAS

The old church clock chimes, 'tis twelve, Christmas Eve,
A cold, soft mantle of snow cloaks the ground,
Young boy, not sleeping, eyes hidden with sleeve,
Waiting for Santa to come on his round.

Long letters to ask of Santa afar,
Best writing of course, and posted last week,
Requests for a plane, a wind-up tin car,
Turreted castle with drawbridge and keep.

Scores of lead soldiers with drums, or a gun,
Some mounted on horses, swords in the air,
To battle for hours, but only in fun,
Time would pass swiftly, with never a care.

Sister wrote Santa a letter as well,
Asked for a pram, complete with a dolly,
Perhaps a new dress, or soap with nice smell,
Or warm woolly gloves for gathering holly.

Letter to Santa from mother did ask,
If only there could be just a small chance,
That all the dads would soon finish their task,
And return home safely again from France.

Christmas morn came, stockings were near empty,
No sign of our dad, toy soldiers or doll,
Just an apple, pennies, hugs a plenty,
The second world war was taking its toll.

John Hoose

CHURCH RALLY

The organ swelled, its music loud
the notes soared high above the crowd
Sunshine filtered through stained glass
with a multi-coloured ray
As if to bless each one of us
assembled there that day
Ladies bore their banner proud
with steps so firm and sure
While members of the choir sang
with voices sweet and pure
On this great day when Guilds unite
and old friends meet again
Co-operation is the word
that forges friendship's chain.

Cecilia Simpson

A LOVE THAT'S NOT RETURNED

A love that's not returned,
is like a letter never answered.
You sit and wait in vain,
To hear that sweet reply.
A love that is not returned,
is like drowning in an ocean.
An ocean made by you.
As you sit alone and cry.

Richard Ball

THE GOVERNMENT

My Honourable Gentleman
Is what he is named,
But surely this is a mocking gesture
And no more than a game.

Passed from one side to another
The private jokes are shared,
Many which are not understood
By the public who often despair.

They lead us and rule us
With so called wit and games,
Which have led us all to think
They are only seeking fame.

Their faces appear on the television,
Their voices on the radio,
But when we ask them a question
Do they answer it? No!

How can we trust them
With our welfare in their hands?
When all they do is quarrel.
Please help us to understand!

Why should we abide by their rules
And listen to their petty fights?
Surely we want a government
Who will give us all our rights!

Rachel Freestone

WAR

Trampling feet marched down our street at dusk,
Mixed with the sweat and heady smells of night,
A mighty muscle of human machine,
Fused into the commands of khaki legions,
Their dropping heads of poignant misery forever watchful,
Only wounded ranks morosely stain the silent street,
Their brooding melancholy shakes the town to wakefulness,
The flares leave the darkness ablaze,
Exhaustion wreaks the stillness of the shells of houses bombed,
And the echo of refugees herded like cattle mingle with the marching,
War leaves its scars,
Full stop, stone dead.

C D Wells

THE WAITING ROOM

I sat there calmly waiting, the seconds ticking by
I wouldn't have to wait too long, I thought between each sigh.

The seconds turned to minutes, I kept glancing at the time,
I started to get restless, and kept praying all was fine.

I'd been waiting for an hour and felt stiff and tired by then,
I got up and walked around and then sat down again.

How much longer must I wait, it must surely be my turn,
My nerves were stretched to breaking, what results was I to learn?

Just when I thought the very worst, and tried not to go insane,
A voice came drifting to my ears, and someone called my name.

D Tinson

DREAMING IN A DREAM

At my own pace and sweet will
Did my soul convince my heart for the very first kill
In at the kill I was to propose to her for a thrilling date
My heart it did tremble with fear and fate
Was I to rest my heart's cry hanging on the sharpest end of time?
My heart it would not agree, and refused to undergo through any more crime!
With this horrifying thought the day turned so blue that it was suddenly a
                                                                                               dreadful night
A blue moon rose which gave my eyes a tender fright
I felt as though *love* had tied me firmly to the cold ground
Now only she and I seemed to be the two lonely souls around.

No sound was then proposed to be heard
Though my eyesight not focused but blurred
I could see her in the distant mist of the dark night
Though she roams the landscape under the virgin light
The love birds sing their own song
And constantly tell me that I am not wrong

She decided to approach me with a smile and in a very slick fashion
Right away my heart granted love and so so much passion
As she approached me, the night was turning into a civil day
With this sudden triumph the place had changed, and we were in a sweet bay
The shine of the star desired to hit her face
Though to me she looked brighter than the star itself!
Now that I saw her I found it difficult to slow down my pace
The beauty my eyeful eyes lived to see was so great,
That my mind was confused and could not work out why I left it so late
With one touch of her irresistible lips
My mind extinguished and erased all extreme emotions of tense
Then *love* decided to run round us and build a heart shaped fence.

Abdul Rob

MY DREAM COTTAGE

I have a cottage in my dreams
Where I would love to live
It's built of stone, and stands alone
With a quiet peace to give
The garden around is full of flowers
Where we can sit for happy hours.

The door with a latch is painted white.
With a coach lamp above to light at night.
As you walk in the door to a hall that's small
The 'Mary Rose' picture hangs on the wall
Then on to a room - a joy to see -
The green carpet, all covered in roses,
With soft comfy chairs
That invite you to sit, an inglenook fireplace.
The fire's always lit!

The windows are pretty with wide white sills.
To hold all my 'Cranberry' collection
And the convex mirror that hangs on the wall,
Takes the scene in with happy reflection.

The kitchen is cosy and all in pine
Full of personal things - especially mine
With a rocking chair for me to sit
While I wait for the supper to cook I'll knit!

And so in the September time of our lives
In our cottage we'll find our peace
'We will enjoy every day'
You will hear me say until life itself shall cease
'Alas'
This cottage in my mind
May prove impossible to find.

Cynthia Shum

IRONED OUT

The endless sleeves
The stiff, ribbed collars,
Pressed into respectability
By my strength, my arm.
My anger, steam and sound,
Pounds this board -
This bored housewife's
Nightmare,
Glare of television, the only sun
In a room boxed smaller
By this raw chore.
To fill these clothes with men!
Pin them to this frame
Crush their legs, slim their bodies,
Apply hot iron to the crutch
And laugh hysterically
At the screams creaking
Through this molten rack.
      Sunday nights
      Puts to rights
      The week's dirt.
      A week's plights
      Sullen fights
      A crisp, white shirt.

Keith Melbourne

THE OAK TREE

I stand and gaze at the old oak tree,
And wonder what tales it could tell,
The times and the changes that it would se,
As on the ground an acorn fell.

When it was planted, it was all green fields,
For company just cows and sheep,
The birds to perch, and eat their meals,
And also to go to sleep.

But now it has changed, they built a housing estate,
But the old tree's still growing there,
She spreads her branches, and grows her leaves,
And in winter she's broad and bare.

I see on her trunk, someone's carved their names,
And a rope for a swing is there,
But she still holds her branches to the sky above,
As if to God in prayer.

I Griffiths

HOME TO ME

North, south, east, west
I've seen the world
and had the best,
The time has come for me to rest
What better place than home to me,
      This England,
A cottage small with friendly walls
that need a coat or two,
A mellow glow and lo behold it starts
to look anew
A welcome fire, a cup of tea, and all
the world's at rest with me,
      A friendly chime comes from the hall
and bids me go to bed,
I snuggle down I'm home at last
and sleep until the dawn
Content to start the day afresh.

Mary Morrison

NO GREATER GIFT

I never told you I loved you.
Yet you, my greatest friend.
But now you've gone and left me
My world is at an end.

You allowed me to be selfish.
You gave me all you had.
And my shame is mixed with sadness
But it made you feel so glad.

I shall never know a dearer love
If I live a thousand years.
And my heart will fill with sorrow
As I shed those many tears.

How could I repay you
If the world were in my grasp?
For you made a wife
Then gave me life.
There's no greater gift than that.

Ken Clifford

ANNIVERSARY

Our wedding day, long time ago
I walked down the aisle
And saw your smile
My heart beat faster, I was all aglow.

I sit alone on our Anniversary Day,
Trying to keep my tears at bay,
Wonderful memories I caress
For you are no longer here I must confess.

Several years we had together
Vowing our love would last for ever,
But memories now are what remain,
Until one day we shall meet again.

Evelyn M Harding

TO A HIPPOPOTAMUS AT MZIMA

You monstrous kind of water nymph,
Performing a grotesque ballet,
Once unseen by all except the camera's eye
But now to a captive audience
Your private life is disclosed.
In the watery depths you sport
With a kind of portly grace,
Bouncing your way, like an astronaut
On the surface of the moon.
Your minions follow closely in attendance,
For your largesse - though crude - is yet life giving,
To all who live in this watery Paradise.
On land, you great lumbering beast,
You champ your way
Through vegetables green and lush
Three hundred pounds - in one night -
Like a great machine devouring.
And yet again, you bob and simper
Among the lily pads,
Rising like some shy maid - your head festooned with lily caps.
But how deceiving you can be, for who would think
That your great rotund body could be moved -
Albeit for short bursts of speed -
At thirty miles and hour.

Lena Brewe

BRAIN JUICE FLAN

Pain makes you yearn,
To learn,
To think,
Then sink,
Then pain starts to gain,
Your hope starts to drain,
Washed away in your fast lane,
 Of thought of sort,
Then caught,
Caught with your broken heart sorrow,
Then pain starts to wane,
And you play the game,
Hard as steel,
Your thoughts start to wheel you,
Back in the fast lane,
So remember,
When pain is pain,
Pain is pain,
But when pain has waned,
You'll have gained.

Mark Underwood

UNFORTUNATE

Reaching out to grab her hand
Frail but filled with sudden life
Relishing with the thought that life is now banned,
Wondering how long he's got his wife.

As tears filled his lonely sad eyes
Nothing left but memories of their love
Heartache is more than he can bear as he begins to sigh
His eyes roam round the room hoping she'll be happy above

Looking down on the face of his wife
Noticing the lines of life endured
Realising every line is a piece of life
Pieced together for one big tour

Pearl drop tears fall steadily downwards
Sobbing loudly in the silent room
Remembering life was filled with love and laughter
Why did life have to end so soon?

As time goes by her hand goes limp
Now the time to lay her at rest
What can I do now he tries to think
But nothing. Nothing can bring life back at a quest

Y Malone

MY RULING PASSION

My ruling passion,
The joy of my heart,
Wakening to the sound of his breathing,
The sun shining down on
His smooth silky body.
His presence controls my thoughts.
The love he gives,
Is so strong,
It rules my mind,
Our hearts pound as one,
But are meant to beat alone,
His love is stronger
Than the world itself.

Rachel Cefai

PARTIES!

Oh I dislike parties, I really do;
the crowds, the milling the fuss and to-do.

Who *are* these people who seem to know me?
'Darling' they call me, and 'Lovey' and 'Dear,'
I'm sure they don't mean it;
they can't be sincere.

But I fear I'm as bad, as you now will see:
('She's aged, she's aged, and her hair's gone white.')
'Ah, Samantha, my dear, how lovely you look!'
(If I told her the truth I'd say: 'You're a fright.')

'Hello there! How nice! It's been quite and age.'
So catty they are, these polite nothingnesses:
'A secret, a whisper, come closer my dear,
but don't say I told you how false are her tresses.'

But now that's enough: I can take no more.
I long for some quiet, I yearn for my space,
I've a pain in my head and I feel rather faint,
the punch was too potent; I'm red in the face.

No I'm *not* very well! I need fresh air.
Oh do please be quiet and leave me alone.
Yes, yes, you go on, but *I* just want *out*,
and peace in my book-lined room, on my own.

Geraldine Squires

SECOND-HAND ROSE

Second-hand Rose dresses up, what a pose,
Looks so good in her coat of fur,
She's paid quite a lot, for the coat that she's got,
But by God, I've got big news for her.

The first owner's dead,
Promptly shot through the head,
You see there's such a demand for his skin -
A magnificent animal, shot in its prime,
Just to Pander to some female's whim!

Lee Chidlow

IN AUTUMN WINDS

Dead leaves of summer blowing in the
wind, left to drift, their beauty gone.
Trees stand naked, stripped of green
now no-one sits beneath their boughs
in autumn winds.

Fields rage with windswept waves
of silver-grey, emptiness reflects from
darkened skies, now no-one lies upon
its green in autumn winds.

Flowers sadly shed petals and bow their
colour-faded heads, left to die their
beauty gone, now no-one walks
amidst their bloom in autumn winds.

Birds gather on a restless murky dawn
ready to take the wing to another
far-away shore now no-one listens
to their sweet and joyful songs in
autumn winds.

It is time to awake from summer's
sleep and bid farewell to our dreams
as they perish and wither like seasons
in the cruel autumn winds.

Graham Roberts

AFTERWARDS

Bitter tears of hot salt fell.
Left hurt to heal and time to tell,
Rippled dreams fade in a wishing-well;
Imprisoned in eternal Hell.

Though smouldering embers burned inside
No comfort came from tears I cried,
And as it was not I who'd lied,
'Twas not my love, but yours that died.

One fantasy now torn in two;
A mystery which gives a clue
Of disbelief in *'I Love You'*
My broken heart, your word untrue.

A fairytale exerting pain
Infests itself within my brain,
Yet gives an impulse to remain,
To hear your 'I Love You' again.

But no repetition came of this,
Two souls returned from single bliss,
From sweet to sour, they shared a kiss -
That held not warmth but prejudice.

So, two hearts against themselves conspire,
And turn all traces of desire
To shattered remnants; once entire.
A unison - now ice, once fire.

Kerri Goodhead

OLD AND DECREPIT

I'm sitting alone
In my little front room
Watching the Tele
And supping my tea

Who cares for me now
That I'm old and decrepit?

I rise early every day
As I used to do
When time meant money
The days were so short

Who cares for me now
That I'm old and decrepit?

The milkman he calls
The paperboy comes
All with no words
Beyond my front door

Who cares for me now
That I'm old and decrepit?

I have my memories
In photos and thoughts
They keep me happy
To die with their words

Who cares for me now
That I'm old and decrepit?

Who cares for me now.
That I'm old and decrepit?

Jane Holmes

THE TWENTIETH CENTURY

The 21st century is now within sight
But of the 20th century what will the historian write
Amazing technology may be a fact
But is mankind any happier for that?

We take for granted electric light
The motor car, radio, TV, the miracle of flight
Advance in medicine can now cure with ease
Many a one-time fatal disease

Benefits to mankind we all realise
But we pollute the earth, the seas, the skies
Rain forests recede with the lumberjack
Animals become extinct in a shrinking habitat

Then reflect on two world wars and the cost
Of the millions dead, the Jewish holocaust
And the media continues to let us see
War, starvation and ethnic cleansing misery

Can we look on this century with pride?
It depends on your circumstances how you decide!
What does a man think when looking back
Whilst living in a shanty town shack?

But just one media picture sums it all up for me
The slaughter of the innocents in this century
A little girl fleeing in pain in Vietnam
Her naked body covered in burns from napalm

K W Benoy

THE TIME OF MY LIFE

I spied a spider, she spied me, my look was fear, hers
was a leer.

Dispelling my doubts, I fought to get out, but she spun and
she won, and my voice wouldn't shout.

My eyes were transfixed, her glare was demanding, the past
should be flashing, account overdrawn, downbeat, forlorn, her
evil intent, my future spent, but those gossamer legs were
truly outstanding.

Caressed by silk, in a web of deceit, tossed and turned,
this way and that, the lull before, canary and cat.

My life-blood was seeping, my tear-ducts were weeping,
then a bug in her trap, became lunch on her lap.

With a crunch of the molars, and a snap of the jaws, the
bottle-blue fly, was thankful to die.

Safe for a moment, not in the frame, then she saw me,
and after 'seconds', she came.

From her gore-covered lips, came a blood-curdling scream,
she pounced for her prize, with a lurch I despised.

As I flailed in her arms, I succumbed to her charms, my
nightmare was over, the dream had begun.

My lovely young widow answers the call . . .

'I'm here sugar-daddy, long legs and all.'

L B Lingard

IRRESPONSIBLE SEA

Do you agree,
that the sea is irresponsible?
For it stretches out its claw,
and sweeps some helpless being under,
tugging them deeper beneath its deceiving surface.
The lifeform gasps for breath,
but the sea continues to drag the person deeper,
it has no pity.
Now the human's lifeless body floats on,
and the sea doesn't care,
no frown,
nor a tear does it shed,
for it knows not what it has done.

Eleanor Clifford (14)

A LIGHTHOUSE SHINES?

When the sun has expired for the day
And its warmth travels elsewhere
Here, I am cold in dismay
Stricken, embalmed in despair.

When my brooding lips of thought speak
As if another is here to listen
Will my words travel hoping to seek
Or can I be sure they'll be lost in their mission?

If my head is to the heavens, so my heart is of the depths
As I glory in the stars to see their wonder manacled.
Vitalise the lighthouse to extinguish wrath!
For constraint leads to one being shackled.

Frankness is bitter when thought is twisted
Sincerity's tongue is ulcered.
What wends furthest unassisted
Blackest heart or pure convulsed?

As the shoulder outweighs the arm of compassion
With stance moulded by its incumbent
Let incubus and the dove meet in equal ration
To live this life in perpetual torment.

If reality is real and I experience pain
Can a lighthouse exorcise time?
Where a cave now inhabits a man
And a man from the depths has to climb.

Steve B

A NEW WAY

My life in the past has been a mess,
I didn't know which way to go
When my guiding angel came along and showed my the way.
A road filled with happiness, love and wonder, a new way
Is this the beginning of a new day?

This angel was a phantom of delight
When it was first I saw her in my sight
She wasn't a real angel, but to me she was.
It is hard to express the feelings I felt
But inside, my heart, I could feel it melt.
She shone with the colours purple and green
The most spiritual colours I have ever seen.

I now realise why my angel is here
Not to take away all my fears,
And not to show me the easy way out
Only to point me in the right direction
And then, it will be, that I will find my way.

Frances Greves (17)

A TIGER'S TALE

On the mantelpiece, in my house,
Sits a tiger, bold and tall,
He sits there, just watching me,
And never moves at all.
His tail is long and very striped,
It hangs beneath the sill,
I like him, he is my friend,
Dare stroke him if you will.

S A Ward

ADRIFT

Can't stand being this free,
You know,
It's so cold out on a limb
Freezing my heart
Till it stops.

I'm swimming with my ship in view
But it's moving,
Not fast;
Nor slow.
Yet they haven't noticed
That out,
I've fallen.

And now I'm swimming
In the deepest water,
Where I could never of imagined I'd be.
I feel,
A loss of security.

Michael Dowd

ENCHANTMENT

The forest is a magical mystical place
The trees reach upwards with such grace
Sounds are changed into things you can feel
Heightened sensuality is so unreal
The magic captivates you, holds you spellbound
From in front of your eyes the mist is unwound
You will begin to see things which are invisible
Creatures of beauty which are not possible
Horses slowly raise up their heads to show
Their beautiful horns with a silvery glow
The magical light reflects in your eyes
More enchanting than stars in the sky
The enchanted dragon sleeps deep in the woods
Waiting for someone to free her with love
People won't own up to the fact that she's there
Finding someone to believe is a magic so rare
The cobwebs of time are draped over her soul
Her heart is an aching unfulfilled hole
People walk past her but alas they can't see
Searching for reasons instead of beliefs
The unicorns play, they're there by the stream
People explain them as some kind of dream
So too are the fairies that dance round their feet
Without enchanting beauty nothing's complete
The forest has cast its spell over me
Within its magic I have been set free.

Clare Hill

UNTITLED

What does Christmas mean to you
Thoughts of home and loved ones too.

Christmas at home with mum and dad
All the things that make us glad.

The Christmas pudding we would stir
And from the woods we'd fetch a fir

Fairy on top and baubles bright,
We ooh'd and aah'd with sheer delight.

Round the fireside in a ring
Christmas carols we would sing.

Jingle bells and socks in a row
Prayers said quick, to bed we'd go.

And o'er the hill, as dawn did peep
Thoughts of a shepherd tending his sheep.

Christmas morn and church bells ring,
Hark the herald angels sing.

The message then of Christmas day
A little child to show the way.

Turkey, mince pies, cake barn-brac,
Xmas presents in a sack.

A game of snowballs in the snow,
Hands a-tingling, cheeks aglow.

Books to read and games to play,
This was a childhood Christmas Day.

Sibyl Smith

ANOTHER TIME, ANOTHER PLACE

When on the edge of deep despair
I cling, uncertain, hesitant,
- A coward, loath to brave the truth
That lurks imprisoned in the mind,
If tumbleweeds of chaos choke
The lifeblood in the veins of thought,
And grief is life, and life is death, -
I find another time and place.

It beckons with a raucous boom
And heals my wounds with stings of salt;
A whiplash from the western wind
Commands the cavalry to storm
And sweep the attics of my mind.
The stampede of a thousand hooves
Soon echoes with a resonance of
Voluptuous velocity.

And years of minutes, squelched within
The quick and crippling hands of time,
Are skeletons inside a grave
That sinks beneath the cavernous depths.
Ashes to ashes, dust to dust.
  I turn to face the morning light,
And railway lines and chimney-stacks,
Then smile because it's Monday.

Sheila Corbett

INFORMATION

We hope you have enjoyed reading this book - and that you will continue to enjoy it in the coming years.

If you like reading and writing poetry drop us a line, or give us a call, and we'll send you a free information pack.

Write to

        Poetry Now Information
        1-2 Wainman Road
        Woodston
        Peterborough
        PE2 7BU